THE LONDON MAGAZINE

EDITORIAL OFFICE

11 Queen's Gate, London, SW7 5EL

Tel   +44 (0) 20 7584 5977

Fax   +44 (0) 20 7225 3273

Email   admin@thelondonmagazine.org

CONTRIBUTIONS to the magazine are welcomed. Submissions by email are preferred. Alternatively, you may post submissions to the editorial office. Only those including a self- addressed envelope, with stamps or International Reply Coupons, will be considered.

SUBSCRIPTION RATES

3 issues   (6 months)   UK £17, EU £20, ROTW £25

6 issues   (12 months) UK £33, EU £40, ROTW £51

12 issues (24 months) UK £59, EU £72, ROTW £92

SUBSCRIPTIONS, RENEWALS & ADVERTISING ENQUIRIES

11 Queen's Gate, London, SW7 5EL

Tel   +44 (0)20 7584 5977

Fax   +44 (0)20 7225 3273

Email   subscriptions@thelondonmagazine.org

         advertising@thelondonmagazine.org

www.thelondonmagazine.org

First published in 1732

Facebook: /thelondonmagazine1732

Twitter: @TheLondonMag

EDITOR
Steven O'Brien

PRODUCTION MANAGER
Heather Wells

REVIEWS EDITOR
Matthew Scott

LITERARY CONSULTANT
Derwent May

SPECIAL EDITORIAL ADVISOR
Grey Gowrie

MARKETING DIRECTOR
Munah Brys

MARKETING ASSISTANT
Jessica Reid

December 2013/January 2014

Ian Madden

One Shrug in Particular

Sensible and slightly hapless to the young foreigner's eye, the teacher's court shoes had obviously been purchased after much deliberation and still weren't quite right. Or so he decided. They were a little tight, yet the way they contained her instep was reassuring.

But what on earth was she talking about?

It hardly mattered; he liked to watch Sugito-*sensei*. Even if keeping up with her was difficult. A diminutive woman in doughnut-coloured stockings and a grey twin-set too thick for the season, she instructed and explained entirely in Japanese.

Though she belonged to the safe, sure days when mistakes were pointed out in your exercise book in thoughtful, omnipotent red, Sugito-*sensei* still had about her the hopefulness of a little girl eager for ticks. Smiling, she gave an abrupt little shrug.

Wide enough for two rows of desks and long enough for a row of twelve, the pebble-grey classroom in which they sat was in an annexe as far from the main entrance as it was possible to get. The room, like the corridor, smelled of floor polish and worn stone – the smells of someone else's school. The walls were unadorned. There was nothing to look at but the teacher with the recently permed steel-grey hair standing in front of the blackboard talking, it sometimes seemed, to herself as much as those she was teaching. Sugito-*sensei* had a large repertoire of shrugs, all of which – or so it appeared – had a subtly different meaning. Some were prim, collected; others almost a shudder. Some were simple, some complex, nuanced. Others were cautious, tinged with diffidence. Yet others, if not transparent, had a meaning which could be inferred. Some were enigmatic (he was sure she didn't mean them to be) and some made the commonplace wondrous.

Of the nine others who had travelled with him from England to this almost metropolitan prefecture – 'Tokyo's bedroom' – to complete the second half of their postgraduate studies, many had been reading and speaking Japanese for a year or more. As this was only his eighth month of learning the language he was, in that sense, the baby of the group. Nevertheless, he could recognise and write two of the three alphabets used in Japan: *hiragana* and *katakana*. Mastering *kanji* – the system based on Chinese characters – was another matter. It was a life's work. Yes, it had been pointed out by the Monday afternoon teacher that the symbol for holiday was, if you looked closely enough, a figure sitting under a tree. Also, little strokes resembling splashes denoted a connection with water. (The calligraphic touches which signified a teardrop and the word for it – *namida* – he found unaccountably beautiful). But there was so much to learn. Too much, perhaps. And it required more motivation than he possessed; or so he was beginning to feel.

Nearest the door sat Jake, bored and haughty, as if hoping to be rescued from the room and his predicament within it. Because the course was new, a hybrid and something of an experiment, its language component was taught at only one level – elementary. This didn't suit Jake. He was a good five years older than any of his fellow students and had been studying Japanese for a number of years. In England Jake had held out for – and had been given – separate tutorials, one-to-ones fitting to his advancedness. No such provision had been made on the group's arrival in Japan. Reluctance on the part of the Japanese university to divide its first ever group of foreigners resulted in Jake having to suffer the indignity of being left among paddlers in the shallow end.

Sugito-*sensei* shrugged again; a more abrupt one this time. All her shrugs were dainty and pleasant, willing her charges to understand. The difficult part was: trying to work out what they might mean and what had given rise to them. Still, he paid close attention to them. They were nearly all he had to go on.

****

That morning's walk to the station had started like any other. He left his host family's house and walked by the dense huddle of scrupulously identical suburban dwellings. All were detached. There was a sliver of space between each house and the next. The vet's on the corner was just opening. Instead of flipping a sign on the surgery door, a life-size model of an Alsatian (alert and open-mouthed and standing on all fours) was placed outside on the pavement. After turning the corner, he went along by the fence parallel to the railway tracks and towards the fizzing lights of the *pachinko* parlour. Its arches of tubular chrome and the over-mirrored interior made him imagine it must be like sitting down to gamble inside a pinball machine.

For the past six weeks he'd followed the same route, down to the minute.

If he had become Japanese in his timekeeping, this had less to do with being in step with the national punctiliousness than with wanting to avoid an unplanned variation. His studies so far had encompassed the country's history, society, constitution and language in equal measure. The part of the course in England and in English now over, the rest was vocabulary and verbs, and finding your way; not just linguistically. With almost every adult prop removed, each day became a succession of tiny but momentous challenges; not getting lost on his way to the university not the least of them.

The abstracted care with which the teacher smoothed down a newly-turned page with the flat of her hand showed respect not just for the book as an object but for the ideas and hard work it contained. Sugito-*sensei* opened it out further and moved her hand across the page in a motion as if giving the knowledge thereon an appreciative polish. He watched. In the absence of understanding her words, her every movement, however slight, was magnified. Her way of handling the book made him feel secure, in good hands.

Part of that day's lesson was about real and artificial. The teacher spoke slowly yet animatedly. Trust the simple, her good-humoured tones seemed to say. She shrugged again. Not all of her shrugs were indecipherable. Some, like the one she just did, had a more prosaic purpose. That last one was a means of ending a digression or of giving notice that she was about to change tack.

The gestures had a quality which made it hard to believe she was a lecturer or professor. At a guess, she had spent her working life with infants and now, close to retiring, she was standing here hoping to be understood. How had she come to be here, one day a week, in front of a disparate clutch of foreigners? It was rumoured that this neat lady without a word of English had been brought in to save face. The English faculty, none of whom had so far risked contact with speakers of the language, were experts content to expound on abstruse aspects of their speciality. And to be spared the potential embarrassments that would surely result from an opportunity to put their knowledge of English into practice. That was where Sugito-*sensei* came in.

When attempting to acquire a language which had an alphabet and root words in common with your own, there was a good chance of deducing what certain lexical scraps meant. This was impossible with Japanese. Sugito-*sensei*'s lesson was like a join-the-dots puzzle. Sometimes he identified a few dots and attempted to connect them. Occasionally he'd be rewarded with a titbit of meaning.

Without the physical idioms of the Thursday teacher he'd have felt even more adrift. They were what he looked to for clues. So far that morning he had gleaned: 'Isn't that a strange rule?'; 'Who knows how that started, but it is so …'; 'I've always liked that …'

The others were scribbling something down. Aware that he was the only one (apart from Jake) not writing, he picked up his pen and started to fill line after line in his notebook. What he found himself writing in thoughtful longhand was thorough. It was painstaking. It was nonsense.

****

The queue at the ticket machines had not been any longer than on previous mornings. But the line he joined turned out to have a high proportion of ditherers. As a result he missed his train by less than thirty seconds. This had never happened before. He waited for the next one. It wasn't long in coming.

Every commuter was reading. Their frowns more intense than any he'd seen on his commutes so far. Several newspapers bore photographs of Sammy Davis Junior. Beside the entertainer's picture were two numerals and the symbol for 'year'. The *kanji* which accompanied this no doubt had a pictorial root but he imbibed the overall meaning without being told. Some knowledge needs no tutelage. It's as obvious as the sky.

On the approach to the station certain buildings – and the blue tarpaulin of the Tinker Bell Visual Café – usually sidled alongside the train, leisurely. Now they were charging by, frantic. In his panic, he got up. No one else did. The train maintained its momentum, ignoring his stop. He peered back pleadingly. The street he should have been walking along in a couple of minutes whizzed past. The roof of the Public House for Enjoyable People and the advertising hoardings above the Snack Captain kiosk were blurs, if that.

He stood by the doors. If only there was an emergency cord which would not only stop the train but make it reverse carefully back along the track. He craned his neck to keep the familiar buildings in sight. But they were gone.

Didn't any of the other passengers want to get off at the station through which they had just sped? It would seem not. They just sat there looking absorbed and grown-up. Or bored.

Helpless, sick – twenty years wrenched from his age in a few seconds – he was being whizzed, mute with his own protests, in the direction of the capital.

One day soon he intended going to Tokyo alone. But he wasn't ready yet.

He was still in the process of becoming attuned to the daily oddities which together would add up, invisibly, to being acclimatized.

Not Tokyo; not today. This morning he had somewhere else to go.

Nipping the material at both shoulders with finger and thumb Sugito-*sensei* lifted it then let it go – plucked it; perhaps to cool herself, perhaps because something was making her uneasy.

'This is real.' Was that what she was saying? 'My hair is real. This is real hair.'

Amazed, she gave the back of her thinning hair a proud pat. Simplifying things over an entire career could have made her a little nutty.

All of a sudden she appeared delighted.

'Hair' was one of the easy words. So were the numbers 'fifteen' and 'twenty-two'. He also heard the words for 'girl', 'village' and 'nearby'. The dots were there but not in sufficient number for him to join them and make sense of what she was saying. One shrug in particular – the one immediately after she touched the back of her head – aroused his curiosity. Delicate, placid and resigned yet the most opaque of the morning's communications, it made him wonder even more than usual about the words her shrugs were meant to supplement.

Sugito-*sensei* was looking directly at him. Without knowing the source of her pleasure, he returned some of it in his smile.

****

It wasn't Tokyo. But it may as well have been. People were bolting – in a severely ordered way – in all directions. Getting off the train, it occurred to him to cross to the platform opposite and wait. But that might be too logical. So he went up a flight of steps and emerged into the purposeful pandemonium of a concourse. There he tried to spot someone who was, if not as disoriented as himself, then at least moving at a pace which would allow an approach. Among the neat, catapulted hoards he caught sight of a young mother with two small boys. She had just passed through the barrier and was tucking her tickets into her purse. One child, about four, was jabbing the other, about five, with a plastic stirrer.

His jaw defiant, the bigger boy kept repeating, '*Itakunai.*'

The woman was still occupied with her bag when, in faltering Japanese, he addressed her. She seemed surprised to be spoken to. Looking to see that the children were within reach, she set about telling him, in English, the platform he should go to.

As the woman was giving directions, the younger child – his cheeks full of air – considered his next move; then dropped a salted plum into the hood of the other boy's sweatshirt. The boy in the sweatshirt retaliated by taking and slowly twisting his tormentor's wrist. Just as the foreigner told the woman he understood, and thanked her, the smaller boy began to cry.

Never quite readied for the tang of tin – coffee in a chilled can remained a cultural bridge too far – he nevertheless sipped the liquid and hoped that before they were due back in the classroom someone would mention what the teacher had been saying.

When gathered round the drinks machine at the end of the corridor, the group would sometimes comment on the morning's lesson, or rather the teacher. The tone of two or three of them never changed. It was that of impatient relevance-mongers. They found the Thursday teacher 'too anecdotal'. Still, if among their complaints they let on what Sugito-*sensei* had been talking about it would save him from having to approach the most advanced of his classmates. He could see it already; the disdain with which Jake would listen; boarding the semi-express not a mistake *he'd* ever make.

Minutes into the break, however, no one had said anything about the lesson.

Either they must have understood every word or, more likely, there were more pressing subjects to talk about. The group was now several smaller groups, each telling of their latest adventures – things still too strange to have become routine.

Unlike the *kanji* on the hurtling train earlier that morning, the teacher's last shrug before the coffee break – the one accompanied by such joy – refused to give up its meaning. There was no way to fill in the gaps with guesswork.

Jake stood scowling out of the window.

There was nothing else for it.

A few yards inside the university gates, he reached up and slapped the cast iron foot of the founder – a vengeful-looking little figure in a wing-collar, his mouth turned down. The likeness gave the impression of being in permanent dudgeon at not having been granted a taller plinth.

He made his way to the annexe feeling like he had been attacked by (and had fought off) something invisible and hostile. He had a sense of having prevailed – he *wasn't* in Tokyo.

The morning had imparted the meaning of a certain ideogram more firmly than repetitive practice with an ink-brush could have done. He doubted whether the symbol would ever separate itself from the member of the Rat Pack it referred to. He suspected that, regardless of what might be covered in class, the mishap on the train would prove to be the day's real lesson.

It wasn't the only thing he'd learned on his way in. Knowing that *nai* when added to a verb made it negative, he now knew – thanks to the little boy on the receiving end of the sugar stirrer – that *itaku* meant 'to hurt.'

He arrived breathless but in time for the start of the first period.

He just came out with it and asked. Stifling a sigh, Jake checked which words his questioner *had* understood. Between swigs from a can of cold green tea, Jake recounted what the teacher had said. 'Fallen out' was a phrase way beyond beginner-level vocabulary, as was 'grow back'. The name of the teacher's girlhood village was something he couldn't have been expected to know either. The nearest city, however, was known to all. Pronounced the Japanese way, according each of its four syllables equal length, it took a second or two to recognise.

That shrug. The corridor lurched with it.

Walking toward the classroom the chatter of the group was as it would have been on any other morning. But now the quietest of their footfalls sounded clumsy. Everything he thought he'd understood about the teacher in the court shoes vanished. The source of her astonishment had indeed been simple. Sugito-*sensei*'s joy, still fresh, was at her baldness having lasted only seven years. Her words – like all words – had equivalents, whether exact or approximate. Not so her shrugs. They remained beyond translation.

Stalker

I have felt your eyes on me before,
But this time their stare is as long and unfocused
As a bat's in the sunlight.
Your eyes skitter and flash
Like minnows in a bathtub,
Caught between my fat thumbs.

I've lived out a of a suitcase for weeks,
I've changed my number,
Moved homes.
But still you find me,
Your eyes outlining my shape
As you peer through blinds,
Round streetlamps,
Into the crates of the moon.

You could find me anywhere.

As a child I got lost in a cave
And I couldn't understand why my cries didn't echo.
Now I know it's because you were there, waiting in the potholes
Swallowing every scream,
Spitting them out again
As silence.

Rabbit Holes

Rabbit-holes that would trip you up
In one faltered outpour of breath
Wait for me in the woods.
Kits slink in the earth below,
My mountainous footsteps rumbling
The little ones who sit up in fear.

But I am no threat: my rubber boots barely break the soil,
Graze nettles tenderly. I step
To avoid being heard.

Many heatless Augusts have passed since I was here last.
Cornstalks wrapped around my ankles,
Cut into the oysters below the bone.
Then I knew no escape,
Had all the isolation of a lifetime packed into a childhood:
To be home was to be alone.

Now I know better; plan my escape routes early,
No need to edge into the hole of a childhood home.
Instead I blink up at the sky, eyes as emptily sightless as the stars.

David Cooke

A Conventional Rebel

The Pleasure Ground: Poems 1952-2012, **Richard Murphy,** Bloodaxe
Books, 288pp, £12 (paperback)

The Pleasure Ground: Poems 1952-2012 is a definitive gathering of
work by a important Irish poet of the Twentieth Century. Born in 1927 at
Milford in County Mayo, Murphy is a member of the poetic generation
whose other most significant voices are those of Thomas Kinsella and John
Montague. While both of these poets have found admirers in the UK, their
first collections were published by the Dolmen Press in Dublin, which
may have hindered their wider recognition on this side of the water. By
contrast, Murphy's first full collection, *Sailing to an Island*, was published
by Faber and Faber in 1963 to considerable acclaim. This was followed by
The Battle of Aughrim (1968), *High Island* (1974), and *The Price of Stone*
(1985). In 1989 Faber and Faber brought out his *New Selected Poems*, but
then dropped him from their list, having shown no interest in *The Mirror
Wall*, his versions of poems from the ancient Sinhalese. It is with a hint
of wounded pride, perhaps, that Murphy recounts in his memoir, *The
Kick* (Granta 2002), that on its eventual publication by Bloodaxe Books it
gained for him the Poetry Book Society Translation Award. Published in
his mid-eighties, *The Pleasure Ground* contains almost everything from
his previous collections with a small number of more recent or previously
uncollected poems. Opening with an autobiographical sketch, the volume
also contains an appendix of documentary pieces giving the background
to various phases of the poet's development. However, disappointingly, it
does not include his versions from the Sinhalese.

Born into an Anglo-Irish family of the 'Ascendancy', Murphy spent
his formative years between Sri Lanka, Ireland and boarding schools in
England. After completing a degree at Oxford he returned to the West
of Ireland, where he ended up earning his living by ferrying tourists to

Inishbofin in a Galway Hooker or *púcán*. The title poem of *Sailing to an Island* is the first, and shortest, of three masterly poems which describe the rugged seascapes and the sailing heritage of Mayo and Galway. From the outset the rhythms are assured and mimetic:

> The boom above my knees lifts, and the boat
> Drops, and the surge departs, departs, my cheek
> Kissed and rejected, kissed, as the gaff sways
> A tangent, cuts the infinite sky to red
> Maps, and the mast draws eight and eight across
> Measureless blue, the boatmen sing or sleep.

Evoking a domain haunted by 'the hot O'Malleys, and the daughters of Granuaile, the pirate queen', Murphy's verse is redolent of local history, Vergilian epic and the realism of J. M. Synge:

> Am I jealous of these courteous fishermen
> Who hand us ashore, for knowing the sea
> Intimately, for respecting the storm
> That took nine of their men on one bad night
> And five from Rossadillisk in this very boat?

An Anglo-Irish Protestant, Murphy is an outsider looking in on a close-knit community, all the more so when he speaks with an upper-class English accent, a fact which we learn from *The Kick* has sometimes been thrown in his face. In two other poems he evokes the figures of outsiders who have come to these desolate parts. In 'Wittgenstein and the Birds' the philosopher is presented as 'A solitary invalid in a fuchsia garden.' In 'Theodore Roethke at Inisbofin' the American poet is another tormented soul: 'laden with books for luggage, / And stumbling under the burden of himself, / He reached the pier, looking for refuge.' In his memoir Murphy explores his patrician background and the tensions between family loyalties and his natural inclination to sympathise with the weak and exploited. Several poems in *Sailing to an Island* are informed by this inheritance. 'Epitaph on a Douglas Fir' is a shapely poem in tercets which develops the Yeatsian theme of the big house in decline: 'Arbour and crinoline have gone under / The laurel, gazebos under the yews;' while in 'Auction' the poet wonders 'With what shall I buy / From time's auctioneers / This old property / Before it disappears?' 'The Woman of the House' is a beautifully sustained elegy in twenty six quatrains written in memory of the poet's grandmother. The exuberance of its imagery is at times reminiscent of Dylan Thomas:

> In the lake of her heart we were islands
> Where the wild asses galloped in the wind.
>
> Her mind was a vague and log-warmed yarn
> Spun between sleep and acts of kindliness;
> She fed our feelings as dew feeds the grass
> On April nights, and our mornings were green.

However, the spare lyricism of 'Girl at the Seaside' hints at the tone of his later poems:

> A sailor kisses me
> Tasting of mackerel,
> I analyse misery
> Till Mass bells peal.

Murphy's ambivalence towards Anglo-Irish history is given powerful expression in 'Droit de Seigneur, 1820', which points towards the historical concerns of his next collection. It is a poem in which the asymmetry between the rights of Gael and Planter is made clear from the start in the poem's title. Evoking the siege mentality of colonists at a time of unrest, it concludes by condemning the injustice of wrongly hanging a simpleton for being one of the Ribbonmen.

Commissioned in 1963 by the BBC Third Programme, 'The Battle of Aughrim, 1691' was broadcast twice in August 1968. In his illuminating note Murphy explains:

I had written enough externally about boats and the sea in *Sailing to an Island*. Now I wanted to look inward at the divisions and devastations in myself as well as in Ireland; the conflicts, legends, rituals, myths and histories arising from possession of the land – why we still had borders and bigotries.

Unfortunately, Murphy's inclusive vision of a united Ireland in a united Europe was soon to be shattered by the renewal of violence in the North. Again, in his note to the poem, Murphy explains how the sequence grew slowly and organically. Written in a variety of stanzaic forms, the poems were then arranged chronologically into four groups: 'Now', 'Before', 'During' and 'After'. A tour de force in which the images are razor sharp, the poet's eye ranges cinematically across the killing fields. 'On Battle Hill' opens with the question that had set the poet on his journey:

> Who owns the land where musket-balls are buried
> In the blackthorn roots on the esker, the drained bogs
> Where sheep browse, and credal war miscarried?

The divisions which survive to this day, enshrined in toponymy, are made clear in 'Orange March': 'Derry, oakwood of bright angels, / Londonderry, dingy walls / Chalked at night with *Fuck the Queen.*' In 'Casement's Funeral', the nationalist hero is placed alongside Wolfe Tone in the pantheon of doomed martyrs. Then, as the narrative develops and we are taken back in time, we see the vanity and incompetence of St Ruth, the commander of the Jacobite forces, who is unable to speak to his troops in any language they can understand. In 'The Sheepfold' the high-handed treatment of some peasants leads to betrayal. 'In Rapparees' the insurgents appear as if from nowhere 'Out of the earth, out of the air, out of the water;' yet the consequences of capture are there for all to see: 'The highway trees are gibbets where seventeen rot / Who were caught last week in a cattle raid.'

It is ironic, perhaps, that having written a poetic sequence which can now be seen as prophetic and a harbinger of Montague's *The Rough Field* and Heaney's *North*, it is at this point that interest in his work starts to wane.

While Murphy struggled with writer's block, the media spotlight was now firmly focused on the violence in the North and the new poets who seemed to be spawned by it. When *High Island* came out in 1974 it contained less than thirty poems, some of which seemed quite slight. However, going back to them now, one finds poems that are amongst the best he has written. Moreover, Murphy's poetry, even at its briefest, has one admirable quality: its memorability. Here are the four lines of 'Double Negative,' originally a much longer poem:

> You were standing on the quay
> Wondering who was the stranger on the mailboat
> While I was on the mailboat
> Wondering who was the stranger on the quay.

Among the highlights of this collection are the five poems about his colonial childhood in Sri Lanka. In 'Firebug' he describes an incident of pyromania:

> The fire bursts into song,
> Eats the doll, stick out its tongue, stands up
> Gyrating like a crimson top: then dies.
> Burnt celluloid leaves a guilty smell.
> The girl cries over the ashes, 'Give me back my doll!'
> 'An angel took it to heaven, didn't you see?'
> The devil needs thrashing with a shoe.

Equally impressive are poems relating to the lives of travelling people. 'The Glass Dump Road' is a dramatic portrayal of child abuse. In 'The Reading Lesson' the poet describes his attempts to teach a recalcitrant tinker boy: 'If books resembled roads, he'd quickly read; / But they're small farms to him, fenced by the page ... / A field of tasks he'll always be outside.'

It was to be another eleven years before Murphy published *The Price of Stone* in 1985. His most substantial collection to date, it was also to be his last. It is divided into two sections: a selection of lyrics in various forms and a title sequence of fifty autobiographical sonnets. Well received on its publication, it showed that Murphy was still capable of writing at the height of his powers. The first section opens with 'Moonshine', an enigmatic love poem: 'I think I love you / When I'm alone / More than I think of you / When we're together.' 'A Nest in a Wall' is less riddling: 'Let me kiss your eyes in the slate-blue calm / Before their Connemara clouds return.' In other poems he focuses upon his day to day life, evoking the rituals of work and community. 'Care', one of Murphy's finest poems, is about a young kid that the poet and some local children killed with kindness:

> Out in a forest
> She would have known a bad leaf from a good.
>
> Here, captive to our taste, she'd learnt to trust
> The petting hand with crushed oats, or a new
> Mash of concentrates, or sweet bits of waste.
>
> So when a child mistook a sprig of yew
> And mixed it with her fodder, she descried
> No danger: we had tamed her instinct too.

Back in the 1950s when Murphy had settled down again in the West of Ireland he bought two sailing boats and became obsessed with their renovation. Subsequently, his purchase of Ardoileán or High Island involved him in a 'mania' for building which he alludes to frequently in his collection of that name and again in *The Price of Stone*. It is appropriate, therefore, that in an autobiographical sequence he should focus on buildings that represent some of the key moments in his life, and that his concern for craftsmanship should draw him to the discipline of the Shakespearean sonnet. Moreover, by personifying each edifice, which then in turn addresses him, the poet is able to put some distance between himself and the life he is examining, while at the same time placing it in the wider context of Anglo-Irish history.

Living for much of his life on the periphery of literary establishments, Richard Murphy is a poet who has gone his own way and transcended the ephemeral. Rightly praised by Ted Hughes for the way his work 'combines a high music with simplicity force and directness,' his dedication to his craft has been exemplary. *The Pleasure Ground* contains a body of work that is coherent, unified, and timeless. It is surely certain to survive.

Peter Abbs

The Rage of Modernism: Self in the Vortex

Who in the world am I? Ah, that's the great puzzle.
Alice in Lewis Carroll's *Alice's Adventures in Wonderland*.

But the truth is that when we write of a woman ...
the accent never falls where it does with a man.
Virginia Woolf in *Orlando*

If I had to imagine a new Robinson Crusoe, I would not place him
on a desert island but in a city of twelve million people.
Roland Barthes in *The Rustle of Language*

To enter the gates of modernism is to tremble, for the landscape that stretches out is vast and various. To begin to describe it is to become immediately aware of another perspective, another contrast, another exception. Yet, acknowledging the complexity, it is still possible to catch some of the salient images and concepts, some of the formative assumptions about the nature of life, and gauge their significance for the story of the self.

I

In a series of lectures given in Geneva between 1907 and 1911, the Swiss linguist Ferdinand de Saussure formulated the principles of a paradigm-shift destined to transform the understanding, even the sensibility, of the twentieth century. The influence of Saussure on language was to be almost as great as that of Marx in economics, Nietzsche in philosophy, or Freud in psychology. His lectures changed the course of thinking in the humanities and had a profound effect on the way the self came to be interpreted. Seldom in intellectual history had so many dry propositions put forward by an academic who had studied the genitive construction in Sanskrit for his doctorate and who was an authority on Phrygian inscriptions and Lithuanian dialects had so subversive an outcome. Even the title of the book, put together by a group of devoted students after his death in 1913 was dramatically dismal: *Cours de linguistique générale*. Yet the book, with its crude text-book illustrations and its lecture-hall odour, had unparalled influence shaping directly or indirectly many of the central assumptions of modernism and, even, postmodernism.

Decades later, it revolutionised anthropology through the work of Claude Lévi-Strauss, psychoanalysis through Jacques Lacan and cultural studies through Roland Barthes. It spawned Semiotics and Structuralism. And, more diffusely, it contributed to a new instability and relativity which began to permeate the Zeitgeist from the time of the First World War. The war marked a disintegration on a massive scale and within its dates we can place the work of the mature Freud and the youthful Jung exploring the unconscious, Einstein's theory of relativity (1916), Spengler's ominous *The Decline of the West* (1918), as well as Saussure's founding of a new linguistics; his lectures were published in 1915. Around the same critical period in the arts we find in 1913 Stravinsky's *Rite of Spring*, Proust's *A la Recherche du Temps Perdu* and Lawrence's *Sons and Lovers* and, in the very first year of the war, Joyce's *Portrait of the Artist as a Young Man*, Kafka's *Trial* and Stein's *Tender Buttons*. Perhaps modernism, defying all definitive explanations, can be best dated from this cataclysmic moment of social destruction and cultural innovation.

What did Saussure's course of lectures propound that was, at once, so inspiring and so disruptive? Near the beginning – and somewhat out of character – Saussure announced his intrepid intention: *A science that studies the life of signs within society is conceivable; it would be part of social psychology and consequently of general psychology; I shall call it semiology.* He went on to unravel the nature of an innovative linguistic science: *Semiology would show what constitutes signs, what laws govern them. Since the science does not yet exist, no one can say what it would be; but it has the right to existence.* This is the voice not of the scholar, but (for one striking moment) of the conquistador and intellectual visionary.

The lectures advocated looking at language under another lens, seeing it at any given moment of time as a self-contained system, requiring no reference to the outside world. *Language is form, not substance*, Saussure declared. To sharpen the analysis, he formulated a distinction between *parole*, the particular act of speech, and *langue*, the grammar determining the manner of its utterance. Saussure gave the masterly example of a game of chess. Any particular movement in chess – the black pawn to square three – would form the *parole*, while the underlying laws of the game – making the move valid or invalid – would be the *langue*. With this distinction it became theoretically possible to detach language from history and the traditional approach of nineteenth-century philology, as also from reference to the outer world which it was traditionally seen as representing, somewhat in the manner of a mirror reflection. In the lectures, language was treated as a complex code, often operating through the inner logic of binaries: light gaining its meaning from dark, male from female, good from evil. The value of any linguistic term was determined by the simultaneous presence of all the other terms in the system, while the relationship between the sound (*signifier*) and the meaning (*signified*) was deemed arbitrary: neither intrinsic nor natural. A sign was not a link between a name and a thing, but between a concept and a sound pattern.

And if Saussure was right, the implications for culture and human identity were huge and hugely unsettling. From the outset of the lectures, the nomenclature approach to language, as ancient as the Book of Genesis and deeply embedded in western essentialist thinking from, at least, the time of Plato, was discarded. From this point, could there be an essential self, integral, true to itself? If there was no logical or natural correspondence between the reality and the sign, analysis must turn to consider *the internal relation between the signs*, to classify the unseen rules determining the movements of the game. *This* was the razor-sharp insight, however partial, calling for a new radical enquiry.

It was Nietzsche who had come closest to the Saussurian revolution and who could see, only too clearly, the outcome for traditional concepts of God and the soul. In *The Will to Power* he wrote with an unsettling perspicuity: *The 'subject' is not something given, it is something added and invented and projected behind what there is ... The subject is the fiction that many similar states in us are the effect of one substratum: but it is we who first created the similarity of these states ... 'subject', 'object', 'attribute' – these distinctions are fabricated and are now imposed as a schematism upon all the apparent facts.* Later, turning his attention to theology, he thundered: *I fear we are not getting rid of God because we still believe in grammar.* Here Nietzsche was striding – in his brilliant impetuous manner – into the then uncharted ocean of semiology. Many of our most cherished beliefs were, he pronounced, the subtle inventions of language. The self enquiring into the self had suddenly fallen, not into the reservoir of being, but into the labyrinth of language. It had become a fiction of the symbolising mind. Thus the death of the subject followed fast upon the death of God. Or so it seemed. Some of Nietzsche's late aphoristic writing marks the very beginning of what was later to be named 'the language turn': that shift to linguistics which played so decisive a role in inaugurating our intricate, plural modern and postmodern worlds.

If some of Saussure's postulates threw a beam of light on the earlier polemical assertions of Nietzsche, they also pointed forward to the philosophy of the mature Wittgenstein, who after the *Tractatus Logico-Philosophicus* (1921) began to insist that it was confusing to think words were connected to reality by semantic links, or that abstract concepts like Beauty, Truth, Goodness or, even, soul and self, denoted stable underlying essences. Although there is no evidence that Wittgenstein ever read the late lectures of Saussure, the two men had much in common. During their lives, they published very little, and their most influential work was published posthumously. Like Saussure (and Nietzsche before him), Wittgenstein argued that the apparent harmony between language and reality was merely a shadow cast over the world by the deception of grammar. One task of the thinker was to illuminate the intragrammatical connections that operated within language: *however, therefore, later, and, but.* Language had multiple uses in multiple contexts and there was no one underlying system on which it rested. Like Saussure, with his example of chess, Wittgenstein developed further the concept of a set of 'language games' governed by different rules. The philosopher's role was no longer to answer the big questions but to unpick the linguistic knots, to undo rather than systematize, to dissolve rather than resolve, to proffer sudden moments of illumination. The acute form of the aphorism returned to the writer's repertoire; not architectonic systems, but the sudden flashes of pure insight, though this shift was somewhat counter to the historical and ideological accents of the dominant modernist spirit.

By the middle of the twentieth century an acute linguistic self-consciousness had materialized. Something of its spirit is caught as early as 1925 in a casual letter of James Joyce to Harriet Weaver. Writing about the composition of part of *Finnegans Wake* Joyce wrote: *I composed some wondrous devices during the night and wrote them out in the dark only to discover that I had made a mosaic on top of other notes so I am now going to bring my astronomical telescope into play*. The perplexed author delights in using 'wondrous devices', in writing upon writing as if literature was a palimpsest, and in the deciphering of unknown symbolic constellations. The orientation is inward, intertextual, self-consciously semiological. It is modernist (and postmodernist) to the core.

Significantly, at some elusive moment, the capital letters traditionally conferred on abstract nouns of value were deemed to be both grandiose and false. The perception ushered in the epoch of the lower case. To the reflexive eye the capitals seemed authoritarian and unconvincing. Such abstractions even called for self-conscious quotation marks: 'justice', 'self', 'soul' – as if the grand encompassing nouns tottered on the edge of collapse, crumbling towers built on epistemological sand. The terms were no longer seen as referring to universal essences or abiding realities, but as 'signifiers' working in the field of language, resonating from previous uses and operating in a variety of different contexts: *'justice' as Plato declares, 'beauty' as Keats avows, 'love', as Barbara Cartland says*. Underlying these small shifts in grammatical convention lurked a number of seminal questions about language, culture and identity. Through the agency of signs did the mind create a *human* world? Did each language – of which there are well over six thousand – construe 'reality' differently? Did the means and manner of formulation shape what was deemed to be descriptively 'true'? Were even the most objective 'data' already in some way coded? Under the dissolving acid of these questions, history could be recast as faction, science as paradigm and art as fabrication (made up of 'wondrous devices.')

One of the more extreme propositions of Jacques Derrida flagged the inexorable direction of the linguistic turn: *Il n'y a pas de hors-texte: there is nothing outside the text* or, perhaps, more accurately, *there is nothing non-textual*. In a similar vein, Roland Barthes, pronouncing the death of the author in 1968 claimed: *Language has no truth except to acknowledge itself as language*. Under the intoxication of Saussurian theory, all notions of an objectivity within a common realm were often absurdly jettisoned as bourgeois fabrications. World and word were falling apart; the falcon could not hear the falconer.

And these unsettling questions and polemical propositions had consequences for the representation and narration of individual lives, for the writing of autobiography, the art of *eudaimonia*. For what, actually, did the tiny pronoun 'I' refer to and what did the noun 'self' denote? Could it be true that the experience of a continuous single identity was, as Nietzsche suggested, a trick of language? In one phase of his life, Roland Barthes certainly thought so and experimented with an anti-autobiography to crown the recognition: a new genre to meet the historic moment of a 'self' which appeared to flounder in the tangled mesh of words and their endless regression into other words. Wittgenstein, too, was uneasy with any concept of a private self, a hidden being with depth, open to introspection or direct analysis. The emphasis, in contrast to the existentialism of Camus and Sartre, fell not on the pang of existence, but on language performing in certain contexts under certain rules. On all sides, a formidable deconstruction was under way. For a time, nothing seemed to have metaphysical or ontological foundations or even, under Einstein's law of relativity, physical solidity.

If the word 'autobiography' was coined by the poet Southey in 1809, at the heights of Romanticism, then a hundred years later, as Saussure was in the very middle of his course of lectures on semiotics, the integrity of the confessional genre was beginning to be doubted. The ethical self was giving way to an ironic self; the singular self was yielding to the notion of multiple roles invented for changing occasions. An individual life was to be read as a slippery polyphonic text open to a multitude of perspectival readings. To talk about 'searching for the self', as if the self were a continuous entity with a unique destiny, was like talking about the sun 'coming up' or 'going down' a hundred years after Galileo. The two thousand year tradition of intimate autobiography, from Augustine to Montaigne to Rousseau, had reached a sudden terminus. Or so it seemed.

II

Implicit in Saussure's semiology was a further angle to 'the linguistic turn' which became equally subversive. If language was not a private, but a collective creation, words could overtake and betray the individual. In each accomodating sentence slumbered a stereotype. Kierkegaard had pinpointed the dilemma in the nineteenth century. In *Fear and Trembling* (1843), he wrote: *Once I speak, I express generality, and if I refrain from speaking no one can understand me.* To speak was to risk becoming a cliché. Without language one was an isolate; but with language one was an aggregate. This posed a real dilemma for the existential writing of autobiography, but there was another aspect to the problem. The inherited freight of language partly concerned ideology.

Political and ethical assumptions were at work in the very act of speaking or writing. To use Nietzsche's terminology, language embodied *the will to power*. In English, for example, 'mankind' ostensibly referring to humanity as a whole, broadcast one half of the human race, while silencing the other. The word was not a neutral counter in a free act of communication, but an assertion of male domination, not immediately apparent. The selective pronoun 'he' to cover both genders reveals the same pattern. In the Oxford English Dictionary the first reflexive meaning of 'self' emerging around 1674, is given as: *That which in a person is really and intrinsically he.* 'She' has no real existence. Language was rarely a transparent medium of equal communication, but more an engine of control, dictating patterns: favouring him, permitting him, and annihilating *her*. But such discriminations, of course, were not confined to gender. The working class in the nineteenth century was often referred to as 'hands': *factory hands, farm hands*. The metaphor carried an assumption, a brutal reduction: those who laboured were no more than manual functions, mere instruments of labour. Similar dehumanising language applied to minority groups, from homosexuals and lesbians, to gypsies, to psychotics, to heretics and visionaries; to any other group whose recognition might threaten the established order.

In his inaugural lecture at the Collège de France in 1977, Roland Barthes, who had extended Saussure's thinking across the whole of popular culture, from striptease to advertising, from wrestling to steak and chips, called language 'fascist': *The object in which power is inscribed, for all of human eternity, is language*. For Barthes speech was classification, and all classification was oppression. Even if his propositions were somewhat hyperbolic – could all language only express power relations? Was not language also poetic and mysterious? And equally capable of love and compassion? – they flagged another critical task that had become a mark of late modernism: the relentless exposing of patterns of domination relating, especially, to class, race and gender. The Sixties gave birth to civil-rights movements, to student riots and sit-ins, to a militant environmentalism, to a whole counterculture of youthful protest across Europe and America. It was the time of the rebel, the outsider, the revolutionary. For many, western culture began to stink; it was viewed as a stinking corpse in need of two things: a handful of quicklime and an instant burial. A hermeneutics of suspicion; a deconstruction of language; an ideological re-reading of western civilisation: these became a crucial part of the Zeitgeist, and have continued into our own time, becoming at times blinding orthodoxies.

Nowhere was the sense of outrage and rebellion more evident than in feminism. After the political triumph of the suffragettes, coinciding with the rise of modernism, this many-stranded movement erupted from all sides: in theology and anthropology, in law and literary criticism, in science and ecology. Often employing the tools of semiology and the insights of psychoanalysis, feminism's searing critique of western culture electrified the impulse to deconstruct and recast, to overthow the dominant patriarchal and capitalist defences, to rebuild the city – sometimes at the expense of aesthetic and spiritual values, sometimes with little regard for the reflexive individual.

Feminist scholars (Simone de Beauvoir, Mary Daly, Elaine Pagels, Marija Gimbutas, Julia Kristeva, Hélène Cixous among many others) exposed the hegemony of the male from Homer onwards. They could explain why in the story of the self there had been such a long silence between the poetry of Sappho and Emily Dickinson; why Plato's philosopher king had no counterpart in a philosopher queen; why there were so many church fathers, but not a single church mother; and why there was such ignorant misogyny in the autobiographical tradition of Paul, Augustine, Dante, Petrarch, Rousseau and Nietzsche. They shed new light on why dualism, based on a rigid system of exclusive binaries beginning with male/female, was *so* entrenched in both classical and Christian thinking.

Once again, the discrimination was registered most dramatically in the 'fascist' formations of speech. Not only in English, but in all the dominant languages of the western hemisphere, the human species had been given an exclusively masculine gender: Greek *anthropos*, Latin *homo*, Italian *uomo*, French *homme*, Spanish *hombre*, German *Mensch*. The pattern of language predetermined the position of women as subsumed, invisible, underneath, there by implication, without a name. In early Greek patriarchal society, Pericles had declared: *The chief glory of a woman is not to be talked of*. As late as the nineteenth century, brilliant women novelists felt they had no choice but to crouch under the powerful mantle of the masculine or indeterminate name: George Eliot, Currer Bell, Georges Sand. The feminists, at their best, revealed how deep and systemic the tyranny had been and the exposure released a torrent of passionate autobiographical writing, from Simone de Beauvoir's *The Memoirs of a Dutiful Daughter* (1958), to Ann Oakley's *Taking it Like a Woman* (1984), to Gillian Rose's *Love's Work* (1995). A two thousand year silence was, finally, broken.

One of the most dazzling literary figures in the early feminist movement was Virginia Woolf. Writing not only experimental novels, but also memoirs, diaries, journals, sketches and letters, she was the intimate reflexive writer *par excellence* – at once modernist in her literary innovations and postmodernist in her recognition of plurality and indeterminacy, but also ranging well beyond such clumsy tagging. All her life she was engaged with the nature of feminine consciousness. At the end of her novel, *Orlando* (1928) she wrote: *When we write of a woman ... the accent never falls where it does with a man.* She was one of the first to recognise the innovative work of Dorothy Richardson, saying of her experimental novel *Pointed Roofs* (1915) that she had invented a sentence *which we might call the psychological sentence of the feminine gender.*

Mocking the mimetic male structures of traditional narratives with their formal railway-line sentences, Woolf aspired to create a genre which might catch the difference of her own acute sensibility. She surveyed the Edwardian male novelists around her – Arnold Bennett, John Galsworthy and H. G. Wells – to judge their work as plodding and literal, moving from a to b to c in a predictable manner lazily inherited from the nineteenth century. They were drab materialists who missed the infinite variety of life, its depth and plenitude. In a new era of relativity, of the unconscious and of semiology, such writing *had* to be out of date; not *modern*; not of the historic moment. In defiance, she sought a fluid syntax which rhythmically enacted the loose drift of daily life, moving at many levels: which flowed like a river, not an urban canal. Like Dorothy Richardson, she wanted her style to be encompassing and polyphonic: elastic enough, she said, to embrace any thing, whether it was solemn, slight or beautiful: thinking in its elementary stage before the rule of logical connectives and semantic stereotypes. The phrase 'stream of consciousness', coined by William James in 1890, anticipated the style beautifully.

Woolf's ideology was as subtle as her style, and her work prefigured much that was to follow in the various feminist movements. Eloquently, she turned the tables over. Like Nietzsche, she recognised that what was proclaimed as history was a testament of power, a tale told by a winner full

NPG x19536, Herbert Read
by Howard Coster
half-plate film negative, 1934

NPG Ax141319, Virginia Woolf (née Stephen)
by Lady Ottoline Morrell, vintage snapshot print, circa 1917

of sound and glory signifying the male ego. When did the decapitated ever give *her* version of events? One of Woolf's tactics to secure equality for women was to take obscure female lives out of the official male dictionaries of biography (her father was the first editor of the *Dictionary of National Biography*) and give them back their lost stories, not as monumental and fossilised figures for the record of high achievers, but as ordinary people in touch with the oscillating rhythms of daily life. In *A Room of One's Own* – a work based on two talks given in 1928, the year when the vote was extended in Britain to all women – she employed another strategy. She brought the art of fiction to bear on the faction of history. Having demonstrated that, although women pervaded western poetry from cover to cover in the stereotypical role of muse, they could hardly read, scarcely spell, and were the property of their husbands, she went on to offer a fictional account of the life and death of Judith Shakespeare, the bard's sister.

Judith Shakespeare had the same encompassing genius as her brother, but was not sent to school and, therefore, had no chance of learning grammar or reading the classical authors. If she wrote anything, it had to be hidden or burnt. She was expected to marry a local woolstapler and when, disdaining marriage, she declined, the spirited girl was severely beaten by her father. At sixteen she ran away from home wanting, like her famous brother, to write and act, but when she reached the playhouse in London she was only ridiculed. Finally, the manager of the theatre seduced her and finding herself pregnant, Judith committed suicide, obscure and unseen. Woolf concluded the tragic biography with a memorable detail. Shakespeare's sister was buried *at some cross-roads where the omnibuses now stop outside the Elephant and Castle.*

Judith is the archetype of the female genius, repressed for centuries, but able to be born again through the labour of women who (in the twentieth century), retiring to a room of their own, might create, as Woolf did, a new symbolic universe of Shakespearean dimensions. The succinct feminist sketch was worth a thousand broadsides of bitter polemic.

Woolf's novels also feature what might be called a postmodern self:

elusive, always changing, multiple and without clear foundations. In *The Waves* (1931) Susan expresses this sense of disorientating inner flux: *For there is nothing to lay hold of. I am made and remade continually. Different people draw different words from me.* Language and identity enmesh but in a diffuse way, not integrating into a single coherent character, but disintegrating into fragmentary parts.

Similar lines of fracture are discovered in Woolf's autobiographical sketches. Her memory struggles to knit together the broken parts, while moments of inner trauma recur to destroy any sense of ultimate unity, any final overarching narrative. The traumatic moments enter unannounced, and leave her in a state of paralysis: *I stood there ... in a trance of horror. I seemed to be dragged down, hopelessly into some pit of absolute despair from which I could not escape. My body seemed paralysed.* Although she saw the process of writing as similar to that of psychoanalysis – on 2nd December 1939 she confided to her diary: *Began reading Freud last night; to enlarge the circumference* – she, assiduously, avoided applying its concepts. Her intuitive intelligence was too fine to be corrupted by the abstractions of theory. She always asked a further question and quietly whispered that reality invariably eluded her. A sensitive diffidence is forever in play: *I could not explain it ... I cannot be sure ... This note is made provisionally ... I have forgotten.* Being pours into non-being; the numinous moment is followed by an annihilating darkness. For each epiphanic memory there is a void of amnesia. As with Dorothy Richardson, there is no grand narrative, only nuanced questions and occasional glimpses of another dimension. But this subtle spirituality was characteristic neither of the Bloomsbury milieu to which she belonged, nor to the modernist movement as a whole.

While Virginia Woolf's autobiographical accounts are profoundly personal and her life, like that of Judith Shakespeare before her, ultimately tragic, they seem to anticipate a new kind of sensibility: polyphonic rather than singular, provisional rather than doctrinal, feminine rather than masculine; subtle, and dispersed. Neither Jungian individuation, nor Freudian realization of the ego, fit the asymmetrical pattern. With one tenacious root in gender, Woolf's work is more mysterious and open-ended. Like Montaigne's

Essays, which she greatly admired, they incarnate a veritable poetics of consciousness. A linguistic reflexivity, a sharp feminist perspective and the power of genius had fused to create a complex vision of personal life: the self as the location of a bewildering, but creative disequilibrium. Woolf's work may finally transcend the conditions of its genesis, but it yet stands firm on the ideological premises of feminism and draws on an innovative culture affirming the supreme value of linguistic reflexivity. It belongs to its period, even as it points towards the postmodern, and beyond.

III

The modernist spirit also has something to do with a peculiar sensitivity to historical time and urban space, with an acute awareness of living in an unprecedented age.

As Saussure was giving his lectures on the new science of semiotics, a revolutionary movement in the arts was proclaimed in the city of Bologna: Futurism. In his 1907 manifesto, the Italian artist, Marinetti, called for an art wedded to the machine: a new aesthetics for the machine age. *A racing car*, he claimed, *is more beautiful than the Victory of Samothrace.* However bizarre the analogy, the thrust of the thought is unambiguous; the art-maker has to embrace modern technology: to look forwards, not backwards. Marinetti wanted archives, museums and libraries torched: *What is the use of looking behind – Time and Space died yesterday – we are already living in the absolute, since we have already created eternal omnipresent speed.* The art of the new century had to express the power of the machine, paint the violent vibrations of the city, capture the furious pace of industrial life. In 1913 a similar movement erupted in London. Ezra Pound, whose modernist slogan was *make it new,* christened it Vorticism. Like Futurism, its purpose was to break ranks with nineteenth century mimetic art by affirming the abstract dynamic of relentless energy. In one of his final meditations in *Ulysses* Joyce had Bloom contemplate *a poster novelty ... reduced to its simplest and most efficient terms not exceeding the span of casual vision and congruous with the velocity of modern life.*

The very word 'modernism' derives from the Latin *modo: just now.* The etymology testifies to the principle of temporality, of living in the immediate historic moment. In 1910 another concept was coined to capture this commitment to contemporaneity: *the avant-garde.* The French word denoting the military vanguard transferred to the arts, now characterised artists and writers as agents of historical change, creative individuals who, militantly occupying the front line, drove events aggressively forward.

Describing the state of art across Europe in 1925 the Spanish philosopher, Ortega y Gasset, wrote: *For about twenty years the most alert young people in Berlin, Paris, London, New York, Rome, Madrid have found themselves faced with an undeniable fact that they have no use for traditional art; moreover that they detest it.* To look back for exemplars was 'reactionary'; to look forward 'revolutionary'. And, clearly, the arena for this revolution in self-consciousness was the city. Marinetti composed his manifesto in Bologna; the young Ezra Pound settled in London; the young Picasso divided his time between Barcelona and Paris. Finishing Ulysses, Joyce proudly added the names of the European centres in which it had been composed: *Trieste-Zurich-Paris* and, self-consciously, then dated the work: *1914-1921.* The dates, spanning the cataclysm of the First World War, bore a special historical significance, while the naming of three cities in three different countries registered the international esprit of the modernist. Taken together, they recorded a trans-national space-time that, by the end of the century, had become electronic and global.

The spirit directing the artistic avant gardes – and there were many – was iconoclastic. For two or three decades there was a cultural efflorescence. It was the aim of the individual to self-consciously embrace historical change; to experiment, to look forward, to leap into an unprecedented vortex of impersonal energies. Addressing an audience of Communists in 1935, the art-critic, Herbert Read, claimed: *Everywhere the greatest obstacle to the new social reality is the existence of the cultural heritage of the past – the religion, the philosophy, the literature and the art which makes up the whole complex ideology of the bourgeois mind.* He ended with three slogans:

REVOLUTIONARY ART IS CONSTRUCTIVE
REVOLUTIONARY ART IS INTERNATIONAL
REVOLUTIONARY ART IS REVOLUTIONARY

The capitalist ideology of the bourgeois mind had to be erased. At first, the art makers thrived on the opposition their work encountered, work such as Picasso's *Les Demoiselles d'Avignon* (1907), Stravinsky's *Rite of Spring* (1913), T. S. Eliot's *The Waste Land* (1922) and Virginia Woolf's *To the Lighthouse* (1927). In America the experimental impulse was given a distinctive voice in the poetry of William Carlos Williams and the novels of William Faulkner. Making it new for them meant working with the beat and idiom of American speech, free from the domination of a senescent European culture.

Movement followed movement, especially in the visual arts, with a dizzy rapidity. But a radical aesthetic based on continuous experimentation and a refusal to inherit was destined to become bankrupt. Perpetual revolution can only end in exhaustion, a staring into the void, all resources discarded, all styles spent. What could possibly follow Joyce's *Finnegans Wake* or Duchamp's *Urinal* or Malevich's *Black Square* or, later, John Cage's *4'33'*? Perhaps, as Nietzsche predicted, the culture of the west had to end with a nihilistic implosion, leaving the self, with no wider sense of belonging or connection, a speck of dust whirling inside the vortex. As always, the existential predicament was best recorded in the more intimate testimonies left by journals and autobiographies.

In his memorable autobiography, *The Innocent Eye*, Herbert Read returned to crystalline memories of childhood in Yorkshire and, significantly, for his epigraph quoted, not Marx nor Bakunin, but Wordsworth: *fostered alike by beauty and by fear*. Once the eloquent champion of modernism, Read, greatly influenced by the work of Carl Jung, felt that his life had been largely wasted by his zestful embracing of a multitude of avant-garde movements. If the creative self was to flourish, it demanded a larger cultural space and a broader arch of time, something more encompassing than the span of casual vision and the velocity of modern life. The past was so much bigger and more versatile than the present. Each section of the autobiography named an objective place in his father's farm: the vale, the green, the orchard, the church, the mill, as if to fix his memory outside the vortex of theory and intellectual fashion. The work is an affirmation of the 'thereness' and 'thatness' of the child's vision, far from ideology, remote from historicism.

In a preface written for the 1962 edition, Read confessed that he regarded the no-man's-land between the two world wars as futile: *spent unprofitably by me and my kind*. The brief, poignant, introduction concluded: *The death wish that was once an intellectual fiction has now become a hideous reality and mankind drifts indifferently to self-destruction. To arrest that drift is beyond our individual capacities: to establish one's individuality is perhaps the only protest*. It was a dramatic act of revision. Herbert Read was urging the individual to take stock; to turn inwards; to reflect backwards. His autobiography can be seen as a modest return to the earlier traditions of autobiographical recreation and the practice of *eudaimonia*. His 'modo' of time had become spiritual and Zen-like, no longer the steel arrow of linear time. Edwin Muir in his autobiography – one of the seminal autobiographies of the twentieth century – likewise expressed a desire to transcend the modernist moment. In the recreation of his life he describes many dreams, and also a sense that his life was a fable; but the time of the dreams and the time of the personal fable, are not fused with historic time. Muir is suggesting that we live, simultaneously, in a number of different times: mythic and chronological, the time of history, the time of the worm and the time of angels. We are the unwitting confluence of a number of different streams of time. The question was not that of simply living in the 'now', but of identifying the stream in which one was immersed. Autobiography with its web of tenses – past, present, future – is particularly equipped to draw attention to the temporal complexity. This is particularly true of Edwin Muir's masterpiece of recall. With *this* poetic recognition of the self as the focal point of diverging threads of time, the modishness of modernism dissolved into an infinitely larger matrix. And so did the concept of the self.

Perhaps, for all its courage, conviction and explosive creativity, the main problem with much of modernism lay in its uncritical alliance with a progressive view of history and the denial of the past tense. Each artist a futurist. The individual became subordinate to the (hypothetical) notion that time was advancing to a grand summation, the apotheosis of the world-spirit or the withering of the state with the triumph of the proletariat. This secular and messianic reading of history derived, of course, from Hegel and Marx, though, in many ways, it was a secular transformation of Christian eschatology. It was a grand narrative saturated with ideology; and was connected to the rise of science and technology after the Renaissance.

From the time of the Enlightenment, these became the dominant paradigm for all knowledge and advance. This was why Freud erroneously considered psychoanalysis to be a science, why Saussure viewed linguistics in the same manner as physics or chemistry and why Jung struggled to hide the occult sources of his thought behind the respectable persona of the empiricist. It was why the Futurists and Vorticists felt compelled to embrace the machine. It was why the individual was often viewed as a passing aberration, a phantom created by the class struggle, which would evaporate as history entered its final stages.

Much of modernism (with a number of great exceptions) was militantly hostile to the spiritual, aesthetic and ethical realm of human life. In this, it represented a flight from the fragility of being and the exacting tasks of *eudaimonia*. The prevailing categories were not ontological, nor metaphysical nor, even, aesthetic; but linguistic, ideological and historicist. In his anti-autobiography, Roland Barthes claimed he would accept any theory showing the self to be 'merely' the effect of language or class.

But Barthes's autobiographical writings never settle; they develop dialectically; they take divergent leaps. Some have regarded him, therefore, as inconsistent, as an unreliable mercurial thinker, even a hypocrite. Alternatively, one can see him as a modern Socrates practicing the *elenchus*, always resisting the comforts of orthodoxy, always turning critically on himself to reach deeper ground: a gadfly for ever changing direction, in search of something more. Strangely, through opening himself to the appalling grief he felt at the death of his mother in 1977, Barthes followed Herbert Read's climactic path moving, at the end of his life, beyond former ideological selves to inhabit a different dimension of existence. In his late work, as we must now see, a reflexive self emerges with a new depth, grace and pervasive melancholy.

Barthes's autobiographical work discloses a dramatic movement from a modernist to a postmodernist stance, to a position (in his very last writings before his tragic death in 1980) that opens up a subjective landscape illuminated by what may be interpreted as spiritual light. Ideology would seem, at moments, to give way to ontology. It is as subtle as it is unexpected: a return to a lost dimension of inner life and a broader concept of time. In the story of the self, his work intimates a dramatic philosophical journey through and beyond the modernist (and postmodernist) Zeitgeist.

In his next essay Peter Abbs will examine the autobiographical writing of Roland Barthes. For further details of the story of the self see:
www.peterabbs.org

Ruth Fainlight

More Ladbroke Square Poems

I

That old tree on the south side of the square is down. In the undergrowth
between the path and railings, where hundreds of daffodils will soon open,
branches and trunk lie cut in lengths: thinner billets of branches, and
from the base of the trunk, disks as thick as elephant feet, each
cut surface raw and pale, and the ground-cover ivy is smeared with
sandy desert-orange-coloured wood-chips and sawdust.

Three children, six or seven years old, two girls and a boy, race
through the shrubs at the side of the path, where the trunk of a tall tree
lies on its side, and the branches, trimmed, lie next to it.
The boy bends to grab one, then calls out:
"Don`t forget that whoever has the stick is the commander!"

II

Inside a yellow laburnum tent
which the rain barely penetrates,
behind a screen of white lilac,
I want to hide.

Queen Anne`s lace and borage
tangle in the foliage
of the lower branches
showering gold and silver petals.

Fallen chestnut blossom
on the pebbled path has

the reddish colour of raw meat
or scabs on schoolboys` knees.

Stooping, I see the fresh
flowers rest on yesterday`s petals:
darkening, softening,
mulching into the gravel.

Almost every bud and frill
of tiny crumpled leaves
crimson and iridescent green
shows the carnal flush of new life:

III

Artichokes with bristling purple thistle flowers
like jaunty cockades on Highlanders` bonnets,
as tall as in my vegetable garden; here
in the square stand formal as gates of wrought-iron.

IV

The square today is full of mothers and children
running and laughing and playing badminton.

Other mothers sitting on wooden benches
talk into their mobile phones and watch the tennis.

A few mothers walk briskly, as if pulled along
the damp gravel paths by their dogs. Almost no one

but me, with anachronistic pencil and notebook,
unnoticed, alone – without a child or a dog or a phone.

V

One September morning
under the willow tree`s green-tasselled tent
that straddled dripping bushes and puddled paths
we sheltered from an equinoctial storm
dragging heaps of yellow leaves across the grass,

then in the empty playground
saw abandoned toys – trucks, buckets and spades,
their primary colours glistening from the sandpit,
jaunty wooden snails to ride like magic horses
and two square swings like small security cages.

The slick shine of rain
makes the metal slide the bed of a river.
Only the roundabout, its bright red struts and
central hub a science-fiction spaceship, hints
that above the cloud stretches endless blue sky.

Derwent May

The Ironical Gaiety of Isaiah Berlin

Building: Letters 1960-1975, by **Isaiah Berlin**, Edited by **Henry Hardy** and **Mark Pottle**, Chatto and Windus, 704pp, £40, (hardback)

Isaac & Isaiah, by **David Caute**, Yale, 335pp, £25, (hardback)

We now have the third volume of Isaiah Berlin's letters, and it is as rich in interest as the two superb volumes that have preceded it. It begins in 1960, the year in which he turned fifty-one. This brilliant son of a Jewish timber merchant, born in Riga in 1909, was by now the Chichele Professor of Social and Political Theory at All Souls College, Oxford, an institution he scarcely knew anything about when he was elected a Fellow of it at the age of twenty-three. He had seen the start of the Russian Revolution in Petrograd, come to England as a boy in 1920, and gone to St Paul's School and Corpus Christ College, Oxford. But All Souls, that assembly of scholars and thinkers whose material needs are provided for, was to be at the heart of his life from then on.

By 1960 he was a famous man. In Oxford he was famous right from his undergraduate days both for his wit and intelligence, and his deep, gabbling voice, which in due course would be imitated by many other young dons. In the country at large, he had won fame for an outstanding series of lectures on great thinkers on the BBC Third Programme. He had also met numerous thinkers, politicians, and writers, and made many close friends. He hated solitude, and when not talking to members of this substantial tribe, he was constantly writing letters to them, often describing and discussing other members of it. It is as if he were a rapporteur of innumerable committees that were engaged in debating the issues of his time, and joining in the debate intensely himself.

In this volume we are plunged in immediately. His spontaneous pen pictures in the letters are marvellous, not least of his Oxford colleagues. Here is a tragic one of the ageing Maurice Bowra, one of his earliest friends in Oxford, and subsequently a renowned, flamboyant Warden of Wadham College. The letter was written to a close woman friend to whom he felt he could write plainly, after Bowra had visited him and his wife in Italy.

> He eats as much as he can: his greed is terrific: & he drinks what he can get: omnivorously & indiscriminately; & grows dark purple: he goes up our hill and down it: slips, falls, takes what Evelyn Waugh called "arsers" – all this can be called intolerable exploitation or great & splendid gallantry, according to one's values: it is both I suppose.... courage: egoism: ruthlessness: like a condottiere at the wrong time and place...I remember how parents trembled at the thought that their sons were being corrupted violently by this Byronic, satanic, brilliant destroyer: now he is a pathetic old porpoise ... a kind of Churchill unrealised.

Nevertheless these letters are peppered all over with admiring and affectionate remarks about Bowra, and in one written after Bowra's death he says, just as spontaneously and sincerely, 'He was a marvellous man, and shaped us all … He was against every kind of narrowness and death'. Berlin's unhesitating impulse to say frankly and wittily whatever is in his head at the time is one of the glories of these letters. It was no doubt helped by the fact that he dictated many of them into a Dictaphone – speaking rather than writing.

The disputes and quarrels between the Fellows at All Souls are also energetically documented – and there were many, especially as the Warden, John Sparrow, was trying to resist any change. The rows came to a head over the wish of Berlin and others to take graduate students into the college, with consequences that we shall see. On the way, we get many more excellent vignettes of people. One notably combative philosopher in Berlin's circle was A. J., or Freddie, Ayer, whose book, *Language, Truth and*

Logic, writes Berlin, 'provoked violent opposition, made happy converts and liberated a large number of people from what they came to regard as metaphysical delusions or prisons. There were a lot of jokes made in 1939/40 about ARP, or Ayer-Raid Precautions.'

Berlin was a deep lover of music, and was for some years a trustee of the Royal Opera House, Covent Garden. This too was a hotbed of disagreements, and Berlin fought fiercely – but with a tact that he could also display – to maintain the highest standards there. In 1965, he says in a private letter that the new Prokofiev Romeo and Juliet 'was an almost indecent success...a kind of highbrow Beatle affair ... One touch of Fidelio or Falstaff by Toscanini, or Don Carlos by Giulini, and all these things shiver into nothing. The ignoble tastes of our most famous and most gifted conductors is a strange and disturbing symptom of our times.'

Oxford, London ... these were places that he loved. But he found other places that welcomed him and where both eye and mind became deeply engaged. He was often lecturing during these years in America, where he had many friends from the period during the war when he was working in the British Embassy in Washington, and made many new ones. He met President Kennedy at a dinner during the Cuban missile crisis ('I had a haircut in his honour'), and was impressed. He tells Bowra that Kennedy 'is constantly alert, never lets go, some kind of electric current moves unceasingly within him and he is thinking political thoughts all the time and never relaxes for one single second'. But Berlin is never really comfortable in America: "They fall in love; then they get into states: the psychoanalyst gets to work; the girls say 'do you have a compulsion neurosis about meals? The boy I go with has a guilt complex about penis envy'". He was happier in Israel, a country towards which he felt a profound but often troubled loyalty. He tells his wife: 'I like the faces, stones, etc. I feel at home, unnervous, unself conscious, don't mind being bored, exhausted, etc ... I don't mind the familiarity, chaos, lack of dignity, noise: nothing is stiff, German, disapproving.'

The political and philosophical ideas for which he became famous naturally appear in many of the letters, particularly when he finds himself called on to defend them. He arrived in Oxford when a variety of forms of linguistic philosophy, such as Ayer's, were in the ascendant, and he made his contribution in that sphere. But he never felt it suited his kind of mind, and he decided to become what he called an historian of ideas – a new concept not wholly welcomed in Oxford, where the tradition was that philosophy was philosophy – an activity of the mind independent of time – and history was history. But it was what he wanted to do, and in due course he wrote outstanding works on the great Russian thinkers of the nineteenth-century, especially Herder, and more generally on the ideas and influence of the writers of the Romantic Age in Europe.

Yet he remained a philosopher in a broader sense. Briefly put, we might say there were two main themes in his philosophical work, and these, which were very dear to him, grew in part out of his historical studies. One was the conviction that sometimes different values, both moral and political, were incompatible. There were liberty and equality, for instance, and you had sometimes to choose between them, and accept the consequences. He did not believe, like many optimistic liberals, that since the eighteenth-century Enlightenment, the world had been on its way to a happy resolution of conflicting human desires.

But he was none the less a deeply liberal thinker. He thought that the widespread kind of liberal mind that believed that human beings could steer societies towards such a satisfactory end was in fact an enemy of liberty. Steering people towards their own liberty, he thought, could end up in their slavery – as it had in the monstrous totalitarian tyrannies of Fascism and Communism.

Out of this belief came the other prevailing theme in his writing – his famous distinction between 'negative liberty' and 'positive liberty'. Positive liberty was when people in power thought they knew best what people wanted, and imposed it on them. Negative liberty was when people could live as they liked, provided that did not interfere with other people's liberty to do the same.

He acknowledged, of course that it was desirable that the state, or society, should provide some things. But he thought politicians should never forget that the purest liberty was 'negative liberty.'

He writes a long letter to the political theorist, Bernard Crick, on these points. It adds to what is in his books and lectures. Crick defends 'positive liberty'. Berlin says freedom means open doors, whereas for Crick it means 'the actual march through them' – something Berlin thinks one should be free not to choose. Berlin imagines a dialogue between Crick and himself …

> "Get out of your corner, stop brooding and realise your personality!" "And if I don't?" "Then I'll jolly well educate you and bring it out, no matter what you want!" "So you will force me to be free?"

In 1963 there was an event that in some degree reflected Berlin's political thinking. Isaac Deutscher, a Trotskyist political thinker, had applied for a job at Sussex University. Berlin, as an adviser to the university board, was asked for his opinion on the matter. Deutscher was turned down. Six years later, a left-wing journal, *The Black Dwarf*, alleged that Berlin had caused Deutscher to be blocked because Deutscher was a Marxist. Berlin was enraged and denied that he had done any such thing. He had a total belief in freedom of speech.

Another new book just out, *Isaac and Isaiah* by David Caute, takes this episode as a basis for a wide examination of the political milieux of both men. Caute, who is himself a former Fellow of All Souls, observes that Deutscher had once written a hostile review of a book by Berlin. He does not directly accuse Berlin of being swayed by personal feelings in whatever he may have said about Deutscher – but the subtitle of Caute's book, 'The Covert Punishment of a Cold War Heretic' suggests something about what he thinks. However, as this volume reveals, in a letter in 1964 to a Polish philosopher, Andrzej Walicki, Berlin writes:

I think that on the whole, Deutscher is the least objective and factually least reliable writer among serious writers on politics to be found today: under the cover of passionate objectivity he hurls poisoned darts into both the left and the right, all except his own tiny faction of Trotskyists and semi-Trotskyists; and has, consequently, one of the least deserved reputations in the world for objectivity, solidity, good judgment.

If that was Berlin's judgment on Deutscher, I think he was right to oppose his appointment at Sussex. Caute acknowledges, at least, that Deutscher would probably not have been happy there.

A letter to another Oxford colleague and friend, Bernard Williams, is one of the most touching in the book, and brings his ideas about incompatible values very delicately into a personal situation. Williams was leaving his wife Shirley, the Labour and then SDP politician, and marrying again. Berlin understands the guilt and agony that Williams is feeling, but says gently that 'conflict is what it is', and there is no way of avoiding it. Williams's guilt and agony cannot be avoided 'save at the cost of some other guilt & agony, or lies, self-deception or patter'. One hopes that Williams, a clear-minded man and distinguished philosopher himself, was helped by the letter.

There was one major change to Berlin's life in 1966 that no-one could have anticipated. He was invited to become the head of a little college – just a converted family house, called Iffley College – for university teachers who were not full Fellows of colleges and consequently had no established home. The argument about graduate students at All Souls was still going on, and Berlin decided that he would accept, and turn Iffley into a bigger college that would house graduate students – especially in science – as well. The letters show the immense efforts that Berlin made to raise money to create it, drawing particularly on his friends in America such as McGeorge Bundy, the Kennedy 'special assistant' who had become President of the Ford Foundation. The Wolfson Foundation was the other main donor, and the fine new building was called Wolfson College. It included, at Berlin's request, an echo of the curved wall in the harbour at Portofino, a place that he adored. The architects subsequently called the block incorporating this feature 'the Berlin Wall.'

Isaiah Berlin unmistakably loved life. Yet there was some deep lack of self-confidence in him that he admits to again and again in his letters. He belonged in many places and yet, in some ways, nowhere. One of the best remarks ever made about him came from the conductor, Robert Craft: an 'ironical gaiety' underlay everything Berlin said. That was perhaps the quality, in both his life and his writing, that enabled him to touch the lives of countless people. It is certainly visible everywhere in this great volume of letters, magnificently edited by Henry Hardy and Mark Pottle.

Anne Chisholm

My London

This is the third in our series in which writers describe what London means to them. Anne Chisholm is a biographer, and Chair of the Royal Society of Literature.

London has always been my true home. The house where I was born, early in World War Two, is a tall grey house by a church on the eastern edge of Regent's Park. These days I often drive past it and while not consciously thinking of her am always aware of my very young mother, awaiting my birth as the battle of Britain was won and the blitz arrived, walking heavily, so she told me, across the road and into the park and across to the Rose Garden, happy, apprehensive, occasionally afraid. When I was a few months old the house was badly shaken by a bomb falling nearby; apparently we were all sheltering in a cupboard under the stairs – my father on leave from the army – but the blast blew the door in and I sustained a scratch on the end of my nose. It left no scar. Soon after this my mother and I left for her parent's house well away from London.

My earliest memories – more impressions or emotions than concrete recollections – all concern the war, for we moved back before it was over to my grandmother's house in Belsize Grove where, perhaps coincidentally, perhaps not, I still live now, although in a block of flats rather than the small white 1830s villa I can just see across the road from my bedroom window. In my building, built in the early 1930s around communal gardens and a swimming pool (long filled in) as the latest fashion in urban living, with a doorman and a restaurant in the basement which would send up meals to order (long defunct, though the former hatch in the wall by my front door is still discernible) there still live one or two very old residents, given to zimmer frames and furs, who arrived from Germany after Hitler took over. One, who gave me coffee and cake after I helped her carry her shopping, remembered firewatching parties on the roof and bombs falling. I think I recall people sleeping in the tube station just across Haverstock Hill; I definitely remember hearing the air raid warning sirens, and being frightened when I was told about the buzzing doodlebugs, which would go silent, cut out and fall abruptly to earth. Ever since, a sudden noise in the sky can make me think of death.

After the war, when we moved to a large red victorian house in Gainsborough Gardens on the edge of Hampstead Heath, Mr Wilmot, the gardener, a stout man in a cloth cap, would take me into his shed and show me a twisted piece of metal he said came from a downed German bomber. I spent hours with Mr Wilmot grubbing around in the bushes. He was a kind man and those were less suspicious times.

Not that my childhood was in the least shadowed by the aftermath of war. I grew up in a comfortable, intellectually inclined, leftish (although my father was always one of nature's Tories and not pleased when I made friends with a Labour MPs family) and confidently middle class Hampstead not yet colonized by the very rich or sprinkled with expensive boutiques. By the time I was nine or ten I was walking alone to school, a long trek to a Catholic convent some way away, chosen by my parents not on religious grounds but because they were told the nuns took girls education seriously. And indeed they did – I owe a lot to the fierce, powerful, clever women who taught me to love Latin (that did not last) and Shakespeare (that did) and made no attempt to convert me, indeed just humoured me when I announced I wanted to be a nun myself and probably in due course a saint.

I would walk back on dark autumn evenings dreaming of sanctity and kicking piles of huge yellow and bronze leaves from the plane trees along the gutters. Each lamppost seemed to have a tall black spear of shadow piercing the foggy darkness above, and the streets smelled of wood smoke and coal dust. There were very few cars about. When I got home I would go round to the back door of our house and often find our charlady, as cleaners were still allowed to be called, cleaning silver at the kitchen table and complaining companionably to my mother about men. I would eat bread and dripping and wonder what they were on about. Sometimes Mrs Wheatley would bring her fatherless son Patrick with her, a solid redfaced boy older than me who would try to squeeze against me on the back stairs. After I mentioned this he did not appear again.

The house was a stone's throw from the Heath, which was familiar territory, with long family walks to Kenwood on Sundays and, eventually, expeditions with friends on bikes or alone with the dog. Once, a pale figure in a raincoat reared up out of the long grass and flashed at me, his limp grey body more pathetic than threatening. Even so I clipped on the dog's lead and ran home with my heart pounding expecting to be the heroine of a drama, to find I was late for lunch, my father was already carving and no-one much interested. 'Don't worry darling' said my mother vaguely, 'That's all they ever want to do.' But later, in my teens, I heard a grim story of a girl who had not got off so lightly.

By that time, though, I was at boarding school in Dorset, where I was happy enough to be one of the relatively few Londoners; most of my friends lived in the country, which then as now struck me as wonderful to visit but no place to settle down. They were all very keen to come to stay with me in the holidays. Home, after the spartan dormitories and bleak communal bathrooms, was heaven, even though in winter I had to jump from bed with my teeth chattering and light the gas fire in my bedroom at the top of the house and jump back before the room warmed up enough for me to face getting dressed. But I could see the dome of St Paul's through chestnut tree branches from my ice-rimmed window (the ice on the inside) and felt all London belonged to me. Teenage life in Hampstead in the late 1950s meant discovering foreign films at the Everyman, hanging around in the one and only Coffee Cup (both still going strong) taking the tube to the West End for a film or a musical (Salad Days, The Boyfriend) or my fathers favourite, a Gilbert and Sullivan opera at the Savoy. As for parties, we put on our shortened bridesmaid's dresses in pastel brocade or taffeta for staid dance in church halls or drawing rooms with parquet floors, with reluctant public schoolboys stuffed into dinner jackets attempting the quickstep. As for sex, even when we were sixteen or seventeen our anxious mothers would ring each other up if anyone was out after midnight, though we went in for nothing more than holding hands and kissing under trees on the Heath, tentatively discovering first love, astonishingly innocent, clumsy and sweet.

Then it was on to university, first journeys to Italy and Greece, my first proper job (after a brief stint on the young *Private Eye*) in New York where one day after about two years my mother, on the phone from Hampstead, asked tentatively if I thought would ever come back to London. I felt a shock of indignation that was almost painful. There was never any doubt in my mind that I would always return to London where I belonged, and when later I found other cities to love – after New York there came Tokyo, Calcutta, Melbourne and Sydney – it was always partly because they reminded me of London, with their endless variety, their secrets, their opportunities, the freedom they offered for reinvention and anonymity, random encounters, privacy in a crowd.

Now, although I am lucky enough to be able to retreat to the country whenever I wish, I recognize that I have no desire to grow old in a village, no matter how peaceful and beguiling, where I would be dependent on the car and observed by kind neighbours. I am best off back home, across the street from the house where my grandmother lived, my sister was born and where I first decorated a Christmas tree as the war came to an end nearly seventy years ago.

Chrissie Gittins

Professor Heger's Daughter

The first came in July when the canopy of leaves
cooled the garden in the afternoon,
she laid the pieces on the table
like islands floating on the green chenille.
Taking paper strips she strapped the words together.
I shall see you again one day ... it must happen since I long for it.
A coral blush rose in her cheeks.

Mother found the second in October,
leaves were crusted then with rust.
She pulled the river tears together with feather stitch,
white cotton whiter than the page,
the thin paper showing Charlotte's
shadow words behind.
– my sisters are keeping well but my poor brother is always ill.

In January, when threads of silver birch were
stained with plum my mother found nine pieces
nestled next to last year's invitations.
If my master withdraws his friendship from me entirely
I shall be absolutely without hope –

Another in November, leaves rotting in the rain.
I loose my appetite and my sleep – I pine away.
This was the last.
I know what it is to love a man and not be loved.
But to see my mother's eyes remember pain?

When my father lay on his deathbed,
his skin wax, his hands clammy and limp,
I flung the letters in his face.
"Did you love her? Did you ever love her?"
He screwed his strength enough to toss them
in the fire.

He found his peace in death.
I keep the letters locked beneath my bed
in a polished leather case.
It's only in the spring I take pleasure in the trees,
I stroke the buds and stems and will the curling leaves
to unfurl into sunlight, to bring a fragrant ease.

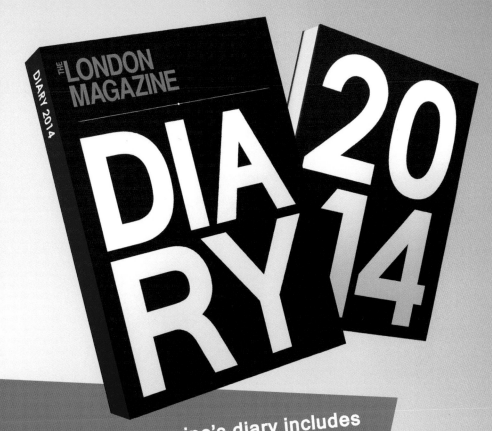

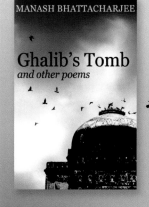

Priscilla Martin

A Generous Correspondent

Remembering Iris Murdoch: Letters and Interviews, **Jeffrey Meyers**, Palgrave Macmillan 2013, 124pp, £30 (hardback)

Jeffrey Meyers met Iris Murdoch and John Bayley in 1978, when he was teaching at the University of Colorado in Boulder and they were invited to give some lectures and seminars at the University of Denver. For about twenty years he corresponded with them. They met again eight times in Oxford and London when he was in England. This book consists mainly of Murdoch's letters to Meyers and finally some brief letters from Bayley breaking the sad news of Iris's descent into Alzheimer's disease. There is an introductory section, 'Remembering Iris', which gives a brief biographical account of the novelist and her love affairs, recalls their meetings and describes his personal impressions of her. The book also includes two interviews with Murdoch and a discussion of the memoirs by her friend A. N. Wilson and her husband John Bayley.

Iris Murdoch was a very generous correspondent with friends, acquaintances and writers of fan mail. By 1964 she was answering ten letters a day. She later told Meyers that she received about twenty every day and, although she produced so much fiction and philosophical work and had no secretary, replied to them all. She thought that some writers of fan mail were lonely and deserved attention. During and after the move from Steeple Aston to Oxford in 1986 Murdoch destroyed a great many letters and presumably few or none of Meyers's to her have survived. Her letters to him are friendly but much less interesting than those collected by Peter J. Conradi for *Iris Murdoch A Writer at War: Letters and Diaries 1939-1945* (Short Books, 2010). Perhaps most people's lives in their twenties are more interesting than their lives after fifty. Murdoch's certainly was and she wrote colourfully and candidly to her dear friend Frank Thompson and her fiancé David Hicks about war-time Oxford and London, her job in the Civil Service and her work with refugees in Austria. During the period of her correspondence with Meyers most of Murdoch's time was spent, very valuably, at her desk writing, though there was social life with friends and travels for holidays or for lectures and interviews. Iris sometimes felt she would be better off at her desk. In 1987 she writes: 'I have been to India, France, Italy and am shortly going to Sweden and then Italy again. Why does[n']t one just stay in one's room and *think*?' And, in 1990, 'I've been away (in Spain) and am about to go away again – why does one do it … ? Staying at home and working quietly is much jollier!' She does not tell Meyers much about her thoughts, though she expresses some predictable opinions: she is glad that the Church of England is ordaining women, sorry that Somerville College, where she was an undergraduate, is admitting men, critical of Islam's misogyny and horrified by the *fatwa* against Salman Rushdie. She is characteristically uncommunicative about her novels. She did not discuss them with anyone, not even Bayley, until they were finished and was very resistant to any suggestions of revision. She continued to read and reread widely and thought *War and Peace* the greatest of novels.

Until we have a *Collected Letters*, which will not be soon, any of Murdoch's available correspondence should be published. But this book adds little to our knowledge of her. Some of it has been published before. The interviews do appear in Gillian Dooley's collection, *From a Tiny Corner in the House of Fiction: Conversations with Iris Murdoch* (University of North Carolina Press, 2003), though slightly abridged, and Meyers, who relates in rather obsessive detail here and elsewhere his editorial problems with their first publisher *Paris Review*, prints them in full and adds (ethically?) some passages which Iris deleted. The content is familiar from Murdoch's other interviews and non-fiction. She speaks of her Irish ancestry, her happy childhood, her early faith, later scepticism and respect for religion, her brief membership of the Communist party, her working methods, the delicate relationship between philosophy and fiction and the moral influence of literature. Meyers's lively Introduction recycles some of the material from his earlier book *Privileged Moments: Encounters with Writers* (University of Wisconsin Press, 2000), such as his entertaining accounts of a characteristically unappetizing dinner at Murdoch's London flat and a party at Steeple Aston. One of the guests at the party, a female ex-colleague with whom Murdoch had an intimate friendship, was Peter (not, as according to Meyers, 'Peta') Ady. The closing section provides a summary of the two memoirs, points out some errors in Bayley's but contrasts Wilson's 'misguided missiles' with 'the healing power of John's fine memoir.' Meyers's own book is clearly a record of a valued relationship with a major writer but does not contribute much that is new to Murdoch studies.

Will Eaves

Winter and Summer

I

Obeying some fond
horrible summons,
as of the dead springing
under the ice,
I pour a kettleful
each morning, gash
their foe, and watch it

squeal with thaw.
Up! Jump! Here!
The spell whitens,
an eye clouds over.
Below it frogs, roused,
glimmer, false dawns
their ritual extremity.

II

Nothing dates like a vision
of the future, but how can we tell

what sort of past is to come?
The autumnal clock in the hall

lined with coats, scarves, Lepidoptera
one pinned wingbeat from jumble –

the clock which, carried downstairs
at a perilous angle, once fell –

instructs no one. A pity. So
many differences are fractional.

David McVey

Sir Walter – the History Man

Sir Walter Scott's work is little read nowadays, yet everywhere there are reminders of his former status. In the twentieth century there was a vogue for naming streets after his works and places associated with him. I grew up on a West of Scotland council estate, in Abbotsford Drive; nearby were Kenilworth Road and Ivanhoe Drive. If you looked out of the back windows you could see Waverley Crescent. In Edinburgh, your train arrives at Waverley Station; close by are the Waverley Bridge, the Waverley Steps and Waverley Gate. Scotland still resounds with the very English name that Scott borrowed for the eponymous hero of his first prose novel.

That novel, *Waverley*, is two hundred years old in 2014, just the latest in a series of Scottian anniversaries; the rollicking verse epic *The Lady of the Lake* reached the same milestone in 2010. These early verse efforts, which also included *The Lay of the Last Minstrel and Marmion*, had made Scott a publishing sensation. *The Lady of the Lake* went viral, and single-handedly began the tourist industry around Loch Katrine and The Trossachs; it's still invoked to pull in visitors two hundred and four years on. Scott's later verse was less successful (who ever reads *Rokeby*?) and Byron was offering tough competition. So Scott switched to prose fiction.

Like many of Scott's works, *Waverley* has a reputation for unreadability, yet this story of a romantically-inclined, ill-educated young English gentleman, Edward Waverley, has some familiar plot elements. Waverley finds himself in the Scottish Highlands during the 1745 Jacobite Rising and struggles to adapt to a people and a culture he simply doesn't understand. Edward Waverley's more recent parallels might include Captain Waggett from *Whisky Galore* and Calvin B Marshall from *The Maggie*. Or, perhaps, TV's *Doc Martin*, with Cornwall substituted for Scotland.

But the novel is far richer and deeper than this caricature of its plot suggests. And in his introduction to the current Penguin edition, Ian Duncan makes the staggering assertion that '*Waverley* has a strong claim to be the most influential work in the modern history of the novel.' This will astonish many and even offend some.

Waverley, as we've seen, is set in 1745; the novel's subtitle is '*Tis Sixty Years Since*, implying an 1805 date of writing. In Scott's introduction to the 1829 Magnum Opus edition, he claimed that the first few chapters had, in fact, been composed around 1805 but, having been found wanting, they were put away in a drawer. He only rediscovered the MS in 1813 when rummaging in the drawer for fish-hooks.

It's a tale that is often repeated in biographies but the facts don't stack up and it feels a bit, well, *fishy*, not least because of the echoes it carries of the story of Scott's 'discovery' of the Honours of Scotland (Scotland's 'crown jewels') in 1818. The baubles had been locked away at the time of the Union in 1707, and turned out to be stored exactly where they were expected to be; but Scott made the most of their stage-managed unearthing. The fish-hooks story reads like a reworking of this.

Many scholars have tried to unravel the actual compositional timetable for *Waverley* and Scott's reasons for creating the fish-hooks creation myth. I think the answer may be simple; an 1805 authorial voice enables the refrain of '*Tis Sixty Years Since*, which flows a good deal better than '*Tis Sixty-nine Years Since*.

Waverley was published anonymously, though most readers either knew the truth or could work it out; Jane Austen certainly had no doubts when she read the novel. The follow-up works – including *The Antiquary, Old Mortality and The Heart of Midlothian* – were credited to 'The Author of Waverley' and became known as The Waverley Novels. They sold in such phenomenal numbers that they put even Scott's verse epics in the shade. He became perhaps the world's first media superstar.

Some commentators in more recent times have not shared this mass enthusiasm for Scott; Edwin Muir's poem *Scotland 1941* put the boot into not only Scott but Robert Burns; 'mummied housegods in their musty niches/ Burns and Scott, sham bards of a sham nation.' More recently, Kevin Williamson, former editor of the ground-breaking Scottish literary magazine *Rebel Inc.,* posted on his blog;

> ... Sir Walter Scott was not a great Scottish patriot nor even a particularly good writer – his prose is stodge – but he was an arse-licking royalist, a falsifier of Scottish history and a Tory c*** of the worst order.

Lest he had not made his point fully, Williamson accompanied his post with a picture of himself appearing to dance on Scott's grave. Classy. Williamson certainly has a point regarding stodgy prose, but everything else he says is either untrue or simplistic. Scott remains perhaps the most successful Scotsman who has ever lived in any field of creative activity, so perhaps there is an element of envy behind Williamson's splutterings.

Broadcasters seem to share the contemporary distaste for Scott; they pushed the boat out for recent two hundredth anniversaries relating to Austen, Darwin and Dickens but not for Scott. At one time his works were regularly mined for swashbuckling Sunday teatime TV drama, but no longer. Oddly, given its colour, intrigue, action and romance, *Waverley* has never been adapted for either TV or cinema.

To understand Ian Duncan's remarkable statement we have to strip away our preconceptions and prejudices about Scott and the Waverley Novels. We see them as old, dusty and belonging firmly to the past, yet in its time *Waverley* was innovative, fresh and original. Its characters inhabit a genuine and identifiable past, interact with real historical events and meet with historical figures. More, they become the means by which Scott examines what is happening in the Scotland and Britain of 1745, and its relevance to his own time.

Re-reading *Waverley* after a gap of around twenty-five years I could certainly understand why some find Scott difficult to get into. In his later novels, Scott used some elaborate and often frustrating narrative framing devices but in *Waverley* there's just a single omniscient narrator and the entire first chapter is an orotund explanation of how the author arrived at his title. There's a whiff of post-modernism here, a self-aware authorial voice, but it is not a chapter that gently eases readers from the iPad generation into the novel.

Subsequent chapters describe the background of the Waverley family and of Edward Waverley. These sections would give a fit of the vapours to any modern Creative Writing tutor who stresses *showing* over *telling*. Then Waverley, though a scion of an old Jacobite family, is packed off to Scotland in the service of the Hanoverian military. The narrative acquires some drive but there's one more snare for unwary modern readers in Waverley's Scottish host, the Baron of Bradwardine, loyal Jacobite and laird of Tully-Veolan. The Baron is a likeable, gentlemanly figure, but Scott makes his conversation pompous and verbose, loaded with legal terms, Latinisms, spurious learning and obscure points of heraldry. You quickly learn to skim-read when the Baron is speaking. He's probably intended as a satirical pop at figures within Scott's circle, perhaps even Scott himself, but the joke falls flat now and probably always did.

The vague and vacillating Waverley warms to the exotic people and culture of the Highlands. After he is mistakenly accused of desertion, he resigns his commission and throws in his lot with the Jacobites. At Stirling and Edinburgh, with the advancing Jacobite host, he meets Charles Edward Stuart himself.

Waverley's desultory education has left him a hopelessly dreamy romantic, hence his beguilement with the Jacobite cause; the same accusation is often thrown at Scott, especially in the way he depicts his country's past. But was his portrayal of the Highlands and its people really a misty anticipation of *Brigadoon*? Here's how he describes the Highland Perthshire village of Tully-Veolan;

> The houses seemed miserable in the extreme, especially to an eye accustomed to the smiling neatness of English cottages. They stood, without any respect for regularity, on each side of a straggling kind of unpaved street, where children, almost in a primitive state of nakedness, lay sprawling, as if to be crushed by the hoofs of the first passing horse.

Scarcely stuff to draw the tourists, and just one of many instances in the novel where Waverley's romantic assumptions and anticipations are punctured.

In the later novels, Scott's narration is more assured, character and scene and plot flow more naturally. In *Waverley* he's still feeling his way, learning the craft of prose writing as he re-invents the Novel itself. All the same, I sometimes recommend people to start reading Scott not with a Waverley novel, but rather with *The Lady of the Lake*. There's no hanging about in *The Lady*; just as much plot and character and incident, but much less wordy flab.

Waverley does grow into an absorbing and thought-provoking read (especially where the Baron of Bradwardine is off the page) for those who persevere and it becomes possible to understand why it matters. Throughout the novel, the phrase 'sixty years since' reappears, echoing the subtitle, and highlighting the differences in Scotland and the UK between 1745 and 1805 (or 1814). In 1745 there is rebellion and discord, nations and communities and families are divided, manners and mores are rougher and simpler, life is harder and shorter.

Scott's narrator represents enlightenment advance and progress, but for Scott the novel is also a warning. In 1814, the Napoleon problem is fresh in the memory (and about to re-emerge) while at home there is agitation by radicals and working-class demands for justice. Scott was an old-fashioned Tory who had little time for radical thinking or social justice. If there is no vigilance, the novel suggests, the present settlement may crumble; capitulate to the lower orders, and the country could descend into the chaos of sixty (-nine) years since.

Even today's most conservative reader would reject Scott's feudal world-view, but this mustn't detract from his literary achievement. Scott used fiction to interrogate the process of historical change and interpret tumultuous events and attempted to portray a nation – two nations – at a painful time when old things are passing away. Scott's prose may hang heavy on the page, lacking the sparkle and wit and style of his contemporary Jane Austen, yet he is harnessing fiction to address matters much weightier than whether some single women can find husbands.

In *Waverley* and other works, Scott's vivid and intelligent portrayal of Scottish history and character helped to preserve a distinct Scottish identity at a time when it was in danger of extinction. Scott's role in the creation of modern tartan kitsch is often condemned; yet there can only be tartan kitsch in a nation that still has some sense of itself, however distorted. Scott helped that sense to survive; he made it cool, if you like, to be Scottish again, albeit within the Union – with preferably no shouting from the working classes at the back, there. More importantly, he had taken the novel into new territory; through fiction it was now possible to investigate history and analyse political change and chance. In Chapter Five, Scott's narrator apologises to the reader;

> I beg pardon, once and for all, of those readers who take up
> novels merely for amusement, for plaguing them so long with
> old-fashioned politics, and Whig and Tory, and Hanoverians
> and Jacobites.

Yet it was that focus that was new and, at the time, exciting. We may reject Scott's Tory view of cultural and historical change, but we must respect the breadth of his historical and artistic vision, and the cultural impact of his work. And nothing had more impact than *Waverley*.

Simone Kotva

Music for the Newer Rite

Incarnation: Music for Christmas, **Thomas Hewitt Jones**, (Regent, 2013).
The Chamber Orchestra of London, Sloane Square Chamber Choir
and Vivum Singers, conducted by Oliver Lallemant. Lyrics by Paul
Williamson and Thomas Hewitt Jones.

'Types and shadows have their ending, | For the newer rite is here', run two
pivotal lines in Edward Caswall's well-loved translation of the medieval
hymn *Tantum Ergo Sacramentum*. The 'newer rite' is a paean to the world
transformed by Christ's death and resurrection; the 'types and shadows'
represent the confusion that precede it: 'For now we see through a glass,
darkly; but then face to face'. Caswall's poetic rendition refers to the ancient exegetical method of 'typology', that is, the tradition of reading the
New Testament scriptures as fulfilments of the Old. St. Paul appears to
have inspired this hermeneutic, explaining to his congregations that the
first man (Adam) was 'the figure (Greek *tupos*) of him that was to come'
(Christ), meaning that just 'as we have borne the image of the earthy, we
shall also bear the image of the heavenly' (Romans 5.14; 1 Corinthians
15.45). In this way Paul wished to graft Christianity to its Jewish stem,
teaching the followers of a new-fangled faith to view themselves as the
most recent flourishing of an historically complex religion. Ephrem the
Syrian, a fourth-century theologian, became an expert exponent of typology, illustrating this method in his *Hymns Against Heresies* as a road stretch-
ing all the way from creation to salvation:

> Smooth to the simple is the way -
> Which is the faith -
> · Which extends lodgings and milestones
> From paradise to paradise,
> [From] which the exit [was] through Adam,
> [To] which the return [was] the robber,
> And investigations, like winding roads,

Have thrown those who have searched
From a smooth to a hard place
(trans. Adam C. McCollum).

Thomas Hewitt Jones's *Incarnation: Music for Christmas* takes its name from its centrepiece 'suite of songs', the latter a deliberate homage to Ephrem's typological method, creating a stirring soundtrack to 'the newer rite' of our own day. The seven-part suite is written for mixed choir, soloists, chamber orchestra, organ and piano, beautifully executed by the Chamber Orchestra of London and Sloane Square Chamber Choir, under the expert direction of Oliver Lallemant. The recording comes out of the ongoing collaboration between young composer Hewitt Jones and writer Paul Williamson, who, with *Incarnation*, have created a sequence of lyrical pieces that play with the familiar themes of the Nativity in a manner which would have done Ephrem the Syrian proud.

In 'Advent', the opening song of the suite, we are thrown back from the present-day anticipation of Christ's entrance into the world (*adventus* means 'arrival' in Latin) to the arrival of humanity at its creation. Our attention is arrested by a rumbling carpet of bass notes, offset by a discordant snaking of diminished fifths in the piano part. This is chaos, the deep *tehom* across which the spirit of God hovered before separating light from darkness. Quickly we pass from this glimpse of the pre-cosmic into a lush tonal score, and hear Hewitt's signature neo-romantic symphonic style in the first rumours of the melodic motif that will be developed at various points throughout the suite. Like a chorus in Classical drama, the choir launches into the first stanza, calling all of humanity to their festivities: 'Come Adam, come Eve, | Come woman, come man … Come stricken and well, | Come, come everyone'. Interspersed among these joyous rallying cries we hear three different responses – three types – to the call of the Divine. Adam 'heard a voice and was afraid', Abraham stands 'prepared with fire and wood', while Mary proclaims, 'Behold the handmaid of the Lord'. The chorus then repeats the first stanza, and 'Advent' concludes on a magnificent fanfare that ebbs out into three pensively chiming octaves, a final echo of the three types at its centre. The scene is set for the unfolding of the next six songs, which together suggest a grand typology between the season of Christmas and the week of creation in Genesis.

After the opening flourish and anticipation of 'Advent', the suite settles into a decidedly darker mood, with 'Falling' and 'Wandering' developing musical motifs from 'Advent' into an unsettled lyricism. 'Falling' alludes to the Biblical Fall and its concomitant Flood, yet here the choir reports The Fall in the thought-provoking type of Lucifer (literally 'the bringer of light'), 'morning's child, | Eyes gleaming in the dawn', who invites Christ to 'freely fall | And choose your mortal shape'. *Kenosis*, the 'emptying out' of Christ's divinity mentioned in Philippians 2, which takes place in order for God to descend into a human form, is here the type which positively corrects Lucifer's own 'antitypical' fall from heaven. In effect, Lucifer is tempting Christ with necessity, as he knows that this particular fall from heaven will lead to a conclusion in the crucifixion: 'Take my hand', he entreats, 'I'll light the way, | We'll dance the dance of death.'

From this incarnational death dance, reminiscent of Ingmar Bergman's use of the Medieval image in his film *The Seventh Seal* (1957), we pass into 'Wandering'. The journey along 'the road to Bethlehem' travelled each year at the return of the liturgical season of Christmas is typologically linked to the exiled Cain, a 'vagabond' who 'hastens eastwards', and calls to mind other archetypal wilderness wanderings: the Hebrews' forty-year Exodus from Egypt and Christ's forty-day temptation. The choir, unaccompanied in a quasi-antiphonal call-and-response, describes Cain's harrowing solitude in the eerily beautiful lines: 'signposts are shifting in the wasteland | trembling on the lifeless ground| Falling like echoes …' As we are led through this landscape of uncertain semiotics, a lone baritone (Samuel Evans), narrating the story of Cain accursed for his wanting sacrifice of first-fruits, is eventually superseded by the re-entrance of the death dance, here in the figure of the shepherds of Abel's assembly, 'with pipes and strings.'

'Nativity', the suite's apex and longest song, is a lullaby with a nod to Elgar and the English Romantic tradition, delivered by the choir to the newborn infant. Its gentle lines are broken up by more sobering interludes that develop the main motif of 'Advent'. In the third and fourth stanzas, after we have been told of the star's 'vigil' over the manger, the choir reflects on those Old Testament types which herald Christ as the wonder of creation. He is both Aaron's rod of the book of Numbers, which blossoms miraculously with almonds, 'a dry stem yielding milky fruit', and the burning bush of Exodus, 'the living flame that's never spent'. Williamson's infant of 'glory infinite' is his mother's joy but also her burden, the conflicted 'youthful conqueror of time', whose victory is simply to have been born. The piece ends on a 'wistful, but overall positive' dotted-quaver variation on the theme of 'Advent', which flows seamlessly into the next movement, 'Planting'. Here choir and orchestra are silenced as a clarinet (Harriet Hougham Slade) and soprano voice (Mary Bevan) intertwine in a mellifluous duet of cadenza-like figurations. The intimate timbre of the two lines, at times blending together almost seamlessly, enhance the typology of this brief interlude, where Christ is 'the seed baptised in rain', the dying and rising god of fertility and recurring bounty. Incarnation means not only the creation of a finite thing, but its establishment in the world as a motif that will itself recur, throughout time. The female voice, the type, perhaps, of a Demeter, a Mary, or a present-day liturgical celebrant, sings this 'lovely tribute to eternity', in which 'time changes' because it returns with 'the rhythm of the year', infinite and open-ended as the dying note on which the song ends.

'Revelling' is a boisterous awakening occasioned by the re-entry of the death-dancers on Twelfth Night, in which the choir ventriloquises the sentiments of secular merry-making in best Dickensian fashion: 'Bring beasts to the slaughter, | Roast turkey and beef, | Baked pastries, steamed puddings … ' Against a rhythmic, fast-paced score, the revellers offer up their goods to their festival's typology: 'The Lord of Misrule'. This is 'Old Noah', who has 'been drinking' and acting the Biblical Silenus, the dichotomy of the plaintive female sower we heard in 'Planting'. Slaughter, harvest and fermentation are the sacrifices which come together in this night of waiting for the events related in 'Epiphany', the final song of the suite. Here we are brought out of the Victorian bacchanalia to the present day, in which the melodic qualities of the 'Nativity' are divested of their ambivalent undertones, unfurling into a score of cinematic tone-painting. As the Magi arrive to attend the manger of the newborn king, the creation-narrative which has been building up over the course of the suite slows to a halt: 'the past year's tale is done and told, | With joy and pain, with rueful smiles and tears'. It is not, however, a restful closure, but an interrogative marker, as the choir asks, 'What story does the future hold | Of ever-changing fortunes, hopes and fears?' And in reply, the final bars of 'Epiphany' are a faintly discordant echo of the initial theme of 'Nativity' played 'as the beginning, reminiscent.'

Incarnation takes us from 'paradise to paradise' in its seven-part Christmas story, sketching out an over-arching typology of creation where the primordial labour of God is typologically mirrored in the labour of Christ to 'fall' into the world and be 'made flesh', thus engaging our own individual struggle with the 'broken wheel' of human finitude and temporality (as we hear in 'Falling'). Ephrem's *Hymns against Heresies* were written in the form of an acrostic alphabet poem, on the theological understanding that anything ordered (as language is) can be a type of the Divine order. Ephrem's alphabet becomes Hewitt Jones's musical idiom, which manipulates themes to allow them to recur cyclically, counterpointing the more narrative typology of Williamson's lyrics.

Williamson's ethos is the 'simple wisdom' to 'Wholeheartedly embrace the day | That chronicles this short-lived time on earth'. Perhaps it is only fitting, then, that the suite is followed by a set of more light-hearted interpretations of traditional Christmas music, balancing the grand themes and more experimental idiom of the preceding songs. In *A Traditional Christmas* Hewitt Jones gives us an orchestral suite consisting of three short medleys of Yuletide favourites in a shimmering score which some may recognise from the Classic FM Christmas playlist. These are followed by *Two Seasonal Carols* performed by Vivum Singers: 'Baby in an Ox's Stall', with Hewitt Jones's own lyrics, and 'Hear the Angels Sing', where Williamson returns as librettist. The tone of the carols, unashamedly crowd-pleasing and 'optimistic' (according to the programme notes), still manages to finish on a note of subtle disquiet. Obscured by the cheerful carolling in 'Hear the Angels Sing' are the lines telling of the manger, where 'watchful lies the Lord of All', returning us, with a jolt, to the double-edged 'infant glory infinite' of 'Nativity.'

The aesthetic of the recorded pieces of *Incarnation: Music for Christmas* as a whole is thus one of a reflective 'modernism', if we may ascribe this term loosely to Hewitt Jones's and Williamson's engagement *with*, rather than rejection *of*, tradition. This modernism might also be the only way to come to grips with the necessary 'contraction' of history into its contemporary expression, as the contemporary philosopher Giorgio Agamben suggests (*The Time that Remains*). In our own age of twice-removed modernity (are we now post-postmodern?), *Incarnation* is a welcome reminder that the unlooked-for which characterises artistic novelty arises not *ex nihilo*, 'out of nothing', but comes to us by way of variation – a non-identical, typological recapitulation of a theme which will always be new.

Norman Buller

G. M. Hopkins, Inscape and Sprung Rhythm

During his lifetime the poems of Gerard Manley Hopkins (1844-1889) had a readership of only a handful of his personal friends. His output was not large; the body of his mature completed verse totals just under fifty poems.

Although his work was produced during the Victorian era his collected poems were not published until 1918, some thirty years after his death. This meant that the work of an obscure contemporary of Tennyson, Browning and Arnold didn't enter the public domain until the early poetry of Pound and Eliot was already there. It is therefore not surprising that Hopkins's poems, regarded as 'difficult and obscure' even among his correspondents, should take their place alongside that of the 'difficult and obscure' modernists.

It is unlikely that any of Hopkins's verse would have survived had it not been for his friend Robert Bridges (1844-1930). The two men had met while undergraduates at Oxford and had corresponded thereafter until Hopkins's death, exchanging and commenting on each other's poems. Although Bridges couldn't cope with Hopkins's originality, stating bluntly that he wouldn't read 'The Wreck of the Deutschland' again for any money, he must have had some inkling that Hopkins's work had merit. Bridges meticulously kept all the manuscripts Hopkins sent to him and, after the latter's death, gradually and guardedly released some of them into publication. Bridges's appointment as Poet Laureate in 1913 enhanced his influence and in 1916 he produced *The Spirit of Man*, an anthology of prose and verse which contained six poems by Hopkins. In 1918 Bridges felt that at last it was time to launch his late friend's collected poems into the public domain.

It took a long time for Hopkins's work to catch on. It was startlingly different from anything produced by his Victorian contemporaries or their successors. About ten years elapsed before all seven hundred and fifty copies of the 1918 edition were sold. Gradually, however, the originality and sheer verbal vitality of his poetry began to be recognised and appreciated, especially among the academic community. Today his work is widely available and critical studies of it abound. Someone once observed that analyses of his poem 'The Windhover' had at one stage become something of a minor industry in the United States.

Gerard Manley Hopkins, the eldest of nine children, was born into a fairly prosperous, middle-class, staunchly Anglican family and grew up in Stratford, Essex, and Hampstead. He was an intelligent child and attended Highgate School from which he won an Exhibition to read classics at Balliol College, Oxford. His life as a student began happily enough but he soon fell victim to the religious doubt that troubled many young Oxford men at that time. Much to the horror and chagrin of his parents, he was received into the Roman Catholic Church by John Henry (later Cardinal) Newman who had followed the same path some years earlier.

Hopkins was all for giving up his studies but Newman wisely advised him to return to Oxford to show that becoming a Catholic had not unsettled him. Hopkins did so and was awarded a Double First Class Honours Degree in Moderations and Greats (classics). Had he remained an Anglican he could well have embarked on an academic career. As it was, his future, to say the least, looked uncertain.

In 1867, the year of his graduation, Hopkins had reached a crossroads. In deciding what to do with the rest of his life he had to take certain facts into account. There is irrefutable evidence that Hopkins was not attracted to women but was attracted to men. He was an extremely devout Christian and there was no way he would ever have put any homosexual propensity into practice. His decision to abandon the Anglican faith was not taken lightly and he did so for what he believed were sound doctrinal reasons. But for him a life of celibacy was essential and it must have crossed his mind that becoming a Roman Catholic priest would satisfy forever any curiosity as to why he did not marry. Having decided upon that course, it was only a matter of choosing which religious Order to join.

Another factor in Hopkins's nature was an asceticism bordering on the masochistic. He had no aversion to being mastered and was willing to surrender his personal comfort and will, indeed his very individuality, to a higher authority. For Hopkins, the stricter the external discipline the more he would be able to exercise the self-discipline needed to trammel and curb his natural desires. Although his own disposition was anything but belligerent, Hopkins had a frank admiration for the armed forces and their personnel and the idea of being a soldier of Christ would have had an undoubted appeal. He therefore chose to join the Society of Jesus, an Order known for its militant practice of Christianity and its demand for unquestioning obedience from its members. He remained a Jesuit for the rest of his life and never deviated from his absolute loyalty to the Order.

As well as for its ardent defence of the Roman Catholic faith, the Society of Jesus had always been renowned for its missionary, educational and charitable work. It was an essentially active movement. It was also thought by many to be philistine in outlook. In general the Society regarded art as an irrelevance which could easily distract its members from their spiritual duty.

In the light of this one wonders whether, and to what extent, Hopkins's choice of religious Order discouraged his development as a poet. It is clear to us today that Hopkins's purpose in life was to produce the poems which no-one but he could write but there was no chance that his Jesuit superiors – or probably even he – would have seen it that way.

From then on his poetry had to take pot-luck among his other demanding duties. This denial of his essential creative self, together with his many other denials, must have caused a chronic drain on his mental and physical strength which, since his constitution had never been robust, set the seal on a life of ill-health, depression and nervous exhaustion. This continued until his premature death just a few weeks short of his forty-fifth birthday. It is not surprising that at the point of his death he was repeatedly heard to exclaim 'I am so happy. I am so happy'. This could only have been because he believed that his soul was being called by Christ, through the Cross, to perfection and that he was at last about to be released from the well-nigh unendurable burden and torment of the life he had deliberately chosen to lead.

The originality of Hopkins's verse is well illustrated by his ode, 'The Wreck of the Deutschland'. It is his longest poem and the first to be written in Hopkins's mature style. He explained how this came about in a letter to his friend Canon Dixon: 'I long had haunting my ear the echo of a new rhythm which now I realised on paper.' Note that the rhythm haunting the ear came before writing the result on paper, which is a clear indication of the priority which Hopkins gave to sound over sight in creating his poetry. He made this abundantly clear in a letter to Robert Bridges: 'Read me with the ears, as I always wish to be read, and my verse becomes all right.'

He called this innovation 'sprung rhythm', 'sprung' in the sense of 'abrupt', since two stressed syllables can occur abruptly one after the other without any unstressed syllables between them. The principle behind it is quite different from that of ordinary metrical verse. In the latter the feet tend to be regular whereas in each foot of sprung rhythm there is one stressed syllable and either any number of unstressed syllables (though usually no more than four) or none at all. The result is an energetic bounding rhythm, rather like a creature of the wild adjusting its step in bounds according to the terrain it is crossing. This is exemplified well enough in the second stanza of 'The Wreck of the Deutschland':

> I did say yes
> O at lightning and lashed rod;
> Thou heardst me truer than tongue confess
> Thy terror, O Christ, O God;
> Thou knowest the walls, altar and hour and night:
> The swoon of a heart that the sweep and the hurl of thee trod
> Hard down with a horror of height:
> And the midriff astrain with leaning of, laced with fire of stress.

Even today this seems a remarkable and unusual way of writing the English language. Imagine its effect on readers accustomed to the soporific tones of the later Wordsworth or the mellifluous cadences of Tennyson!

Coleridge asserted that poetry gives most pleasure when only generally understood. Regarding this poem, Hopkins remarked in a letter to Bridges:

> Granted that it needs study and is obscure, for indeed I was not over-desirous that the meaning of all should be quite clear, at least unmistakeable, you might ... have never the less read it so that lines and stanzas should be left in the memory and superficial impressions deepened, and have liked some without exhausting all.

This was another instance of Hopkins pleading for his work to be read with the ears, for its musical structure to be accepted as meaningful, leaving the mind to catch up later.

What was it that made Hopkins feel it was essential for him to write in this way? It stemmed from his belief, which was also that of the medieval theologian Duns Scotus, that every created thing, from a mere stone to a human being, was literally inimitable, a one-off, in essence quite unlike any other. It was this factor, the sheer individuality of anything, which he sought to discover in whatever he encountered, including, as in part one of 'The Wreck of the Deutschland', his own personal life experience.

Hopkins called this quality 'inscape'. When he was moved to express this in verse he sought to choose and arrange words in a way which best represented his experience of that unique essence. This meant forcing language to work extremely hard in the pursuit of this aim and if the current conventions of language needed to be sacrificed to that end, so be it. The result was often the compact, hard-edged, multi-adjectival, exclamatory, battering verse which, at its most successful, miraculously achieved a lyricism and beauty all its own and rarely equalled by others.

Hopkins had an interest in music throughout his life and he set to music poems by Shakespeare, Sappho and others, including verses by his correspondents Bridges, Dixon and Patmore. Little of this, it seems, has survived. It is likely that this interest in music found its truest expression in his verse structures, for these show an unmistakable musical presence which, far from being merely ornamental, is an integral part of each poem.

Hopkins's poem 'Spring and Fall' is a good example of this musicality. It also shows that sprung rhythm doesn't always have to be intense and flamboyant.

Spring and Fall:
To a young child

Margaret, are you grieving
Over Goldengrove unleaving?
Leaves, like the things of man, you
With your fresh thoughts care for, can you?
Ah! As the heart grows older
It will come to such sights colder
By and by, nor spare a sigh
Though worlds of wanwood leafmeal lie;
And yet you will weep and know why.
Now no matter, child, the name:
Sorrow's springs are the same.
Nor mouth had, no nor mind, expressed
What heart heard of, ghost guessed:
It is the blight man was born for,
It is Margaret you mourn for.

Various conjectures have been made as to the identity of Margaret or whether she really existed at all. Hopkins merely commented in a letter that the poem was 'not founded on any real incident'. For some eighteen months during 1880 to 1881 Hopkins served as priest at St. Francis Xavier's church in Liverpool where he found his duties generally uncongenial. Occasionally, however, he was sent by train on a more welcome task to Rose Hill, the estate of a Catholic family near Lydiate in rural Lancashire. There he would stay the night and conduct Mass before breakfast on the following day. He explained in a letter to Robert Bridges how the poem 'came to him' on the morning of 7th September 1880 as he walked to the railway station on his return to Liverpool and he was able to send the completed poem to Bridges only three days later. Exactly what inspired the poem will probably never be known but it seems most likely that the young child Margaret never existed and was a fictional notion invented by Hopkins for the sake of the poem.

In this fifteen-line lyric the overall structure is neatly arranged, the first six lines in three rhyming couplets, and the last six also, with a rhyming triplet in between. Rhythmic unity is maintained by each line consisting of four sprung rhythm feet having four irregular stresses per line.

Hopkins, not being a North American, obviously chose the word 'Fall' in preference to 'Autumn' for its ambiguous meaning of both the descent of dying leaves and the Fall of mankind. This ambiguity is essential for understanding the poem, taking the reader into the heart of the Garden of Eden in the Book of Genesis and reminding us of the opening lines of Milton's *Paradise Lost* where 'Man's First Disobedience ... Brought Death into the World, and all our woe.'

The title immediately presents a contrast between the two different and opposing conditions of spring and autumn. This also suggests, by metaphorical association, the contrasts of youth and age, innocence and experience, freshness and decay and purity and corruption.

The poem ostensibly addresses Margaret, the young child in the subtitle, though this can only be a rhetorical device since it is unlikely that any real child would have been able to grasp the significance of the poem. If we accept the fiction which the poem offers, it seems that Margaret has made it known that she is saddened by the mass death of the falling leaves. The name 'Goldengrove' indicates a place where trees (grove) bear dying (golden) leaves but it also meets the poem's requirements regarding rhythm and sound. It is known that there were at least two landed properties of that name in or near areas where Hopkins had lived.

The poem begins by examining, in the first four lines, the girl's reason for weeping. Several ideas and threads of meaning are introduced and skilfully woven together and the unusual, crabbed syntax is the result of their considerable compression. The expression of grief at the death of leaves by a child (who could well be approaching adolescence) must seem to an adult mind out of all proportion to the ostensible reason for it. The implication is that she is experiencing, albeit subliminally, a truth far more profound than the death of leaves. The phrase 'things of man' is used to imply maturity as distinct from childhood, experience contrasted with innocence, corruption compared with purity, autumn (Fall) as distinct from the 'fresh thoughts' of spring – indeed, the whole paraphernalia of the adult world and its awareness of what is euphemistically called the 'facts of life.'

That all this should have been made available to the attentive and responsive reader in only the title and first four lines says something about the quality of the language with which we are dealing. The ability to achieve such precise suggestiveness and concentration with such musicality has been given to few writers in the history of the English language.

The Book of Genesis has it that Adam and Eve lost their perfection and immortality by activating sex and death in disobedience of God's decree. Thereafter sex and death would be mankind's fate forever and so Margaret, despite her present innocence, is destined to experience the Fall's consequences also. As she approaches adulthood, ('as the heart grows older') she will become inured ('come to such sights colder') to the death of leaves because she will become conditioned to man's fallen state and be part of the corrupted world.

In line eight the words 'wanwood' and leafmeal' are examples of how Hopkins would create new words in pursuit of the precise expression of 'inscape'. For 'wanwood' he was clearly after a word which would combine the qualities of 'wan' – dark, gloomy, discoloured, sickly, waning – with 'wood' – an area of trees. Similarly 'leafmeal', after the fashion of 'piece-meal', combines 'leaves' with 'meal', i.e. falling one by one and eventually crumbling into a fine texture.

The line 'And yet you will weep and know why' is pivotal to the poem. The implication is that the adult and mature Margaret, with her heart grown older, will certainly have plenty to weep about but, because no longer in a state of innocence and wholly involved in the process of original sin, she will be fully aware of the consequences of the Fall and therefore will 'know why' she weeps.

Lines ten and eleven advise the child not to concern herself with particular reasons for sorrow, such as dying leaves, because all sorrow stems from that one momentous cause which 'Brought Death into the World, and all our woe.' For someone of Hopkins's beliefs, no greater deprivation for mankind than the Fall could even be imagined. Lines twelve and thirteen assert that in her present state of innocence the child Margaret would find it impossible to utter (mouth) or even think (mind) what her heart was inarticulately aware of and her spirit (ghost) had subliminally surmised.

The final couplet sums up the significance of Margaret's sorrow. In seemingly mourning the mortality of falling leaves she is really mourning the mortality of fallen mankind, 'the blight man was born for'. Since her spirit (ghost) has 'guessed' her implicated in the Fall, the girl's mourning the death of leaves is only ostensible and she is subliminally mourning for Margaret, her own fallen self.

Stuart Henson

After the Dance

For Margaret McMahon

He will come when the grasses
have given up their lights
and hogweeds darken against the sky.

He will come when the bats are plying
the arch of the copse
with their black, sporadic flight.

He will come when the woodbine
breathes its unbearable
sweetness adrift on the night

and long down the lane by the close
where the hedge-shadows drown
he will listen and wait.

He will fetch me home to the last barred gate
in the speechless dusk
as if it were not too late, too late.

Lana Asfour

The Allure of the Pearl

Pearls, **V&A and Qatar Museums Authority Exhibition**,
21 September 2013 – 19 January 2014

Pearls, on exhibition currently at the Victoria and Albert Museum, elegantly reveals the long historical allure of these precious objects. At once dispelling myths about nature's formation of pearls and demonstrating the skills – and indeed mortal dangers – involved in diving for and trading them, the exhibition presents the sophisticated taste and craftsmanship that has gone into setting and displaying them through a spectacular array of jewellery and clothing dating back to antiquity. Implicitly, the exhibition imparts a lesson in human vanity: appreciated for their rarity and beauty, the value of pearls has been connected with symbolic and religious power but it has also been inextricably bound with extremes of worldly power and wealth.

Indeed, the pearl has arrived at the V&A accompanied by the latter, since the partner for this exhibition is the Qatar Museums Authority (QMA). The QMA's head, Sheikha Mayassa bint Hamad bin Khalifa Al Thani – the thirty year-old daughter of the Emir of Qatar – has been referred to in the press as the most powerful woman in the art world who controls an enormous budget for investment in art. Although it is not made officially public, the British media has speculated on her annual budget, and this exhibition underscores the grounds of those speculations with some extraordinary items.

From antiquity to the mid-twentieth century, the Arabian Gulf was one of the main sources of pearls with Qatar and Bahrain at the centre of the pearl-diving industry. From there, pearls were traded and sent to Europe and Asia via the Indian Ocean. Pearls have also been found in many other areas, including the Philippines and Burma, the Caribbean and Solomon Islands, Mexico and Peru, North America and New Zealand. But it was only with the emergence of cultured pearls in Japan in the early twentieth century and the spread of modern pearl culture techniques that the precious jewel became affordable to many more consumers, modernising its appeal. By the mid-twentieth century, the pearl-diving trade in the Arabian Gulf had ground to a halt and many natural pearl sources around the world had begun to dry up.

Nevertheless, the decline of pearl diving coincided with the discovery of oil in the Gulf. This has made Qatar one of the richest nations in the world, boasting the third-highest GDP. The QMA holds the world's largest collection of natural pearls as well as some very valuable pieces of natural pearl jewellery. Qatar's recent investments in art are turning the small nation into a regional cultural centre, though some of its purchases have caused controversy and have been seen as inflating the art market. Last year, the QMA notoriously paid $250 million for Cézanne's *Card Players*, the highest sum ever paid for an artwork. Another recent purchase is the 1930s Cartier five-strand natural pearl necklace with diamond and platinum clusters, bought from Sotheby's for over £2 million and displayed amid the panoply of other treasures at the current exhibition.

Qatar's investment drive, which includes education and culture more generally, is explicitly justified as a way of preparing for a post-oil economy. But it may also be seen as part of a wider nation-building project, legitimizing the young gulf nation, which remains an absolute – if enlightened – monarchy during a period of instability and revolutionary upheaval in the Middle East.

Beatriz Chadour-Sampson, curator of the exhibition, understandably avoids discussing the wider political and economic issues, and declined to comment on the effect that such a large budget may be having on the art market and indeed on museums such as the V&A. Her focus is the exhibition itself, and rightly so, since it commands attention on its own terms, whatever the socio-economic context of the international art market and its wealthiest investors.

Pearls happily adheres to classical aesthetic principles by being both pleasurable and instructive. Based on the 2010 and 2012 exhibitions in Doha and Kobe respectively, which focused on the natural history and scientific formation of pearls, *Pearls* has received the best of V&A treatment by taking a different path. It journeys though the history of pearls, allowing audiences to gawp in wonderment at their sensual beauty in fashion, state costume and jewellery since Roman times, through the Byzantine era, the Middle Ages, Renaissance and beyond, right up to contemporary times, both in Europe and further afield.

The exhibition begins with a short but fascinating lesson in the formation of pearls, dispelling the popular myth that pearls are formed around a grain of sand. It shows instead that pearls are created when a parasite intrudes into almost any sort of shell or mollusc. The parasites are usually tapeworm larvae that inhabit and are excreted by sharks, pikes and other fish. When they enter a mollusc, they disrupt the cell growth between the shell and its lining, or mantle. Nacre cells grow around the parasitical worm, often encasing it until it dies and disintegrates, forming a pearl.

After the science, another short section on pearl diving reveals the simple techniques that were used, unchanged, for centuries. A video made during the 1970s by Qatari television shows one of the last pearl diving expeditions along the Qatari coast. The exhibition then takes the visitor on the historical journey through fashions in jewellery and clothing. Portraits of queens, duchesses and aristocratic ladies decked in pearls are included, as are drawings of jewellery designs and pearl-encrusted clothing. The majority of the exhibition, though, consists of pearl jewellery and accessories, ingeniously displayed in solid but attractive nineteenth-century metal safes. Chadour-Sampson explained that these safes belong to a designer who lent his collection to the V&A when the insurance company demanded secure displays for the treasures.

The jewellery is certainly fabulous and begins with fine examples from the Roman and Byzantine empires. In medieval Europe, the pearl was associated with power and authority and was used in coronation regalia and

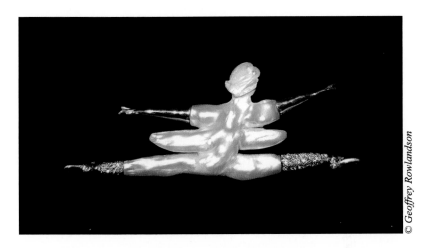

Grand Jeté , gold with diamonds and two cultured baroque pearls
Geoffrey Rowlandson, London 1999

Necklace, natural pearls from the Gulf with platinum and diamond clasps
The Qatar Museums Authority Collection, 1930s by Cartier

Photo © Creutz

A rare selection of natural pearls from the Qatar Museums Authority Collection
The Qatar Museums Authority Collection

church silver. It was also associated with Christ and the Virgin Mary and symbolized purity and chastity. On display is a rarely seen medieval jewelled girdle with animal motifs lent by New College, Oxford. The pearl has often symbolized sensual beauty, purity and fertility, and has been associated since ancient Greece with the goddess Aphrodite, who was born from the foam of the sea.

Rather poignant is Charles I's pearl drop earring. An authenticating letter written by his grand daughter Mary II tells us that this was removed from his ear after his head was severed at the executioner's block in 1649.

During the Renaissance more widely, the irregular shapes of 'baroque' pearls encouraged goldsmiths to create fantastical pendants and bodice ornaments, turning the pearls into parts of animals, ships and human bodies. Hence we see an Italian pendant with a lion standing on a snake, and a lively carnival dancer, whose body is a large baroque pearl.

The eighteenth and nineteenth centuries, meanwhile, saw pearls used in 'sentimental' jewellery, with pieces representing love or mourning. Victorian items include pearl-encrusted watches and brooches carrying intimate messages, and naturalistic designs depicting vines, fruits and flowers. Remarkable pearl and diamond objects include the Dagmar necklace that belonged to the fashionable Princess Alexandra of Denmark who eventually married British King Edward VII, and the large moth and spider brooches that belonged to Empress Eugénie of France, who also inspired the fashion among European aristocracy for wearing multiple long strings of pearls. Historical events often play a key role. The emergence of new bourgeoisies created increased demand for pearls and diamonds, and European revolutions led to the sale of toppled monarchs' collections. After the collapse of Napoleon III's empire, for instance, the French government sold the Crown Jewels in 1887. These were bought by Parisian jewellery houses and Tiffany in New York, and sold on to aristocratic ladies or to new industrial and financial elites.

As we move into the twentieth century, art nouveau pieces include extraordinarily shaped baroque pearls set into pendants, as well as long necklaces like the 1925 Cartier *sautoir*. A section on 'authority and celebrity' shows pearls intricately sewn into the clothing of Indian nawabs or decorating Russian icons, while later on pearls are prominently placed in the tiaras of European aristocracy or symbolically decorate a ball gown worn by Queen Elizabeth II on a state visit to France. The visitor can also delight in the large natural pearl drop earrings designed by Bulgari that belonged to Elizabeth Taylor, or the simple string choker of cultured pearls bought for Marilyn Monroe by her husband Joe DiMaggio, which she wore on the day of their divorce.

The final section is dedicated to the cultured pearl, pioneered by Kokichi Mikimoto in Japan in the late nineteenth century. An illuminating two-minute video demonstrates Mikimoto's grafting techniques and there are some impressive exhibits of early and contemporary Mikimoto pearl pieces. Also on display are pieces of jewellery made from cultured South Sea pearls, found in a surprisingly vast array of colours that reflect the colour of the shells in which they are found; these are loaned by jewellery designer Yoko, and followed by some highly original pieces by contemporary designers.

The exhibition ends by questioning about the future of cultured pearls, with a display of buckets filled with mass-produced Chinese pearls. While China does produce some high quality salt-water pearls the vast majority are of mediocre quality. Since mussels are resistant to pollution and as many as fifty grafts from a donor mussel can be inserted into each one, freshwater mussel farms can be created in any watery area, including flooded rice fields and near housing estates.

What is missing in *Pearls* is some sort of comparison with other jewels, such as diamonds, emeralds and rubies. I found myself asking whether this kind of treatment of pearls through the ages could be applied to any gemstone. A detailed comparison would undoubtedly require another exhibition, but a general statement of what Chadour-Sampson told me independently would have been useful: while the value of and fashion for diamonds, emeralds and rubies throughout history has depended on when and where sources have been found, pearls are a 'global phenomenon' which have been continuously in fashion because they have always been found – and found throughout the world.

The book that accompanies the exhibition provides far more information than the exhibition itself. It is more than a simple exhibition catalogue and begins to answer some of the questions about the cultural history of pearls that the exhibition leaves open. Nevertheless the exhibition stands admirably on its own and the V&A has brought its expertise in the history of jewellery, fashion and design to this particular subject. With two hundred objects from forty different lending sources, both institutions and private collectors, it has added breadth as well as symbolic and historical perspective to the original Qatari exhibition.

Anthony Head

Mortality and Dream ... and a Love of Good Books

I sometimes wonder what book I would read if I knew it were to be my last. *Candide* would be an immediate contender, as would *A Glastonbury Romance* (and not just to stretch out the time). Possibly some essays of Montaigne or Primo Levi. But perhaps I would settle for Rabelais or a volume of P. G. Wodehouse and just die laughing. It was a topic among many my friend John Vernon and I used to discuss, exchanging titles and enthusiasms. When it came to it, he had been re-reading *Paradise Lost* with renewed amazement, and had also found pleasure in returning to the Attic Greek textbook of his schooldays.

One thing I can't discuss with him now is a peculiar dream I had.

There comes a tipping point in life – in any life lived to a natural extent and not truncated by tragedy – where the number of departed friends, or just the old familiar faces, begins to outweigh the number of those who remain to us. I haven't reached that stage, but John's departure set me counting back again through the years, and brooding on the enduring strangeness that our 'allotted' spans should be so various and on the randomness of our fates. I thought of Angus, here in Tokyo, walking normally one day and starting to stagger the next – prelude to the discovery of a tumour in his brain already so big as to be inoperable; of his devastated girlfriend Kayoko, engulfed a few years later by a tidal wave on a beach in Sri Lanka; of my bubbly grandmother Rosa, who lived a healthy life throughout an entire century, just touching the two either side of it; of easy-going Sally, who had little more than three decades before cancer took her from her daughters.

In such recollections old university friends loom large. My Selwyn College contemporary Chris Foale lost his life a year after graduation in a car crash in Yugoslavia (from which his brother Michael miraculously emerged and went on to become the first Briton to walk in space). Others who had slipped away I learned about through obituaries encountered later by chance: the scholar Siobhan Kilfeather in Belfast, the poet Anne Blonstein in Basel – two more still youthful victims of cancer.

At times it's the injustice that impresses, at others the absurdity. A year ago my Czech friend Otakar, who had been looking forward to a well-earned retirement with his wife in Prague, succumbed to *The Talented Mr. Ripley*. A sensitive and loving man, he was so upset by the film of Patricia Highsmith's story that no sooner had he switched off the television than he began to suffer palpitations. As his wife went to the phone to call an ambulance, he unwisely tried to stand again and fell, cracking his head in the process and inducing a fatal haemorrhage.

John had made his living in the financial field, dividing his time between Britain and Japan, a country to which he responded with the true discrimination of the connoisseur and critic. We had come out to Japan together many years earlier as English teachers and he had eventually relocated to London with his Japanese wife and daughter. Later, when settled in the purlieus of Purley, with an MBA from the London Business School to add to his Oxford degree, and having had his fill of working for banks, he had set up his own financial training venture.

But his heart was less in finance than in literature and history. He read widely and thoughtfully. He would write reviews of books and send them off a dozen at a time by email to selected friends, works that ranged from Marguerite Yourcenar to Patrick O'Brian, from Don Cupitt to Dorothy Hartley, sometimes with a favourite classic thrown in – *Gawain and the Green Knight* or his beloved *Tristram Shandy*. I urged him to send some reviews to various journals, but he could never be bothered. Eventually he took to posting some online, but it was discussion with friends he most enjoyed, the sharing of ideas and loves in conversation rather than the hasty and fragmented discourses typical of cyberspace. When we last talked on the phone, he had said he was looking forward to Forrest Reid's *Demophon*, a magical Greek fantasy, which my small press was planning to republish. But his long – and for so long, so secret – struggle with myelofibrosis was nearing its end, and two weeks later it was pneumonia that brought the *coup de grâce*.

John had nothing but praise for the nurses and doctors at the south London hospital where he had spent so much of the last year. But he had been under no illusions about the chances of surviving his bone marrow transplant. He researched the whole business with the thoroughness of a statistician, which rendered somewhat feeble my attempts to encourage alternative visions of reality. But philosophically he had most of the bases covered. He knew his C. S. Lewis and his Richard Dawkins too, his Buddhist interpreters and his Zen koans. In recent years he had become acquainted with all three of the Powys brothers – with the psychological profundities of John Cowper, the no-nonsense epicureanism of Llewelyn, the melancholy mysticism of Theodore. He was especially struck, as all its readers are, by the chapter titled 'The Dirt of God' in the latter's *Kindness in a Corner* in which the sexton Truggins allays the fear of death of the elderly Mr and Mrs Turtle with a comically emotive enactment of the blessings vouchsafed for us by a grave in a country churchyard. It is one of the most extraordinary passages in our literature – one which induces in the reader, as with the Turtles them-selves, a curious longing simply to lie down and die. Not that John had any intention of doing so. I had wanted to get Nicolas Berdyaev's *The Divine and the Human* to him too, as a kind of counterpoint, with its marvellous definition of immortality as 'memory made clear and serene', but reluced lest it had seemed precipitous, an admission almost of defeat. In any case, it would have required more energy than was left to him.

During one of my recent visits home, when he had still been just well enough to drive, we had met in Winchester. As the autumnal drizzle grew heavier in the late afternoon we took refuge in the Cathedral, joining the thinly scattered congregation and adding our voices to 'Praise, My Soul, The King of Heaven', as if both trying to recapture something that time and distance had left behind us, something specific to each of us yet somehow unifying. We took in again some of its many monuments – the great west window, an abstract masterpiece formed of the glass that was shattered by Cromwell's batteries, the Fishermen's Chapel with Izaak Walton's memorial, the mortuary chests of the Saxon and Danish kings, the gravestone of Jane Austen that breathes no word of her writings but honours the woman and friend. When we parted outside, I tried to resist the feeling that this would be my last sight of John, as he walked slowly away with the aid of his stick, tall and thin in his trench coat and wide-brimmed fedora. It proved not to be: prosaic as reality is, that was of John in hospital later in the spring being suddenly wheeled off down the corridor for yet another scan. But it remains my valedictory image, the one that abides.

And then he came into my dream on the day of his funeral. It was a very brief scene, one among many in the usual hotchpotch of these emanations from our nether-consciousness, or as some would have it, from the spirit world. It was a scene as if from a silent movie. In a small, bare room, John was sitting in an armchair, with his back to the camera, as it were. I had the feeling I was standing behind him with one of my hands on his shoulder, while stroking his head with the other, as if in an act of reassurance. This sense of the tactile was very strong, yet I had no visible presence. To his left sat our mutual friend Luke in profile, and next to Luke in another armchair sat an unidentified man in a black cassock and dog collar. His face was not known to me or even distinct, but I had the sense after waking that I had somehow been introducing John to this friendly stranger.

I thought no more of the dream for a while, but recalled it some days later when speaking with Luke on the phone. He related how when he had last seen John in his hospital room, two days before he died, a priest had entered to deliver a Bible. The padre of the local parish apparently did the rounds of the hospital, though I had no knowledge of this, or that John had spoken with him on an earlier visit and accepted his offer of a copy. But there these three men had been, in a room together, two of them old friends of mine and the other an unknown man of the cloth.

It's unusual for me to dream of specific individuals I cannot identify, and it was only in mentioning this to Luke that I added what was, in fact, the most puzzling element of the dream for me – that this stranger had been a black man. Luke's silence was eloquent, and when he spoke again it was to tell me that the padre was from Kenya.

Most dreams are bizarre and their contents unaccountable, though often one can recognize components and make obvious associations. But some cry out for rational explanation. The only explanations I can think of for this one are beyond rationality. To attempt to 'interpret' it would seem to me to cheapen whatever significance it may have. So I content myself in embracing the mystery of its irrefutability, and in satisfying the desire to record it.

Perhaps, after all, the 'Good Book' was the last one John had been reading. That too would have been a return to his roots, emotional if not intellectual. I will like to think it was John who was reassuring *me*, conveying to me this singular scene in the only way left when letters, emails and phone lines are gone. 'Blessed are they that mourn, for they shall be comforted.' Or to give it the Rabelaisian form: '*Bon espoir y gist au fond*' – Good hope lies at the bottom.

A Hologram of the Holy: Bridging the Cultural Divide

One of the most enlightening encounters between two faiths occurred in the thirteenth century when St. Francis of Assisi journeyed behind the lines of the battlefield at Damietta, Egypt, during the ensanguined onslaught of the Fifth Crusade. It was there that he met with the Sultan Malik al-Kamil who in the course of a fruitful dialogue offered to bring Francis to a mosque. Francis accepted, adding an observation that should unsettle dogmatists who have deflected from the core commonality among religions: 'God is everywhere.' Or as his contemporary the Sufi Muslim poet Rumi put it, 'Even though you tie a hundred knots, the string is one.'

On a psychological level, this transcendence of ecclesiastical divisions may be seen as a perennial expression of what William James in *The Varieties of Religious Experience* referred to as the personal experience of God beyond 'institutional' religion.

It may also be understood as a manifestation of a primordial archetypical repository of universal spiritual experience elucidated by C. G. Jung as the collective unconscious. We may think of the image of the mother Mary, a symbol of the feminine guide to the higher realm of the spirit in both Christianity and Islam. It was not long ago that Pope John Paul II referred to Muslims as 'brothers' and, only a few months after his election, invoked 'Mary Queen of Peace' in the Lebanon conflict, pointing out that she is venerated by both Muslims and Christians alike. Pope Francis has in the spirit of his namesake, with humility and prescience, symbolically expanded this rapprochement by washing the feet of a Moslem woman on Pentecost, the first time in papal history that either a woman or Muslim was included in the ritual begun by Christ, 'What I have done is set you an example, so that what I did you may do likewise.' (John 13:15)

The return to this primal source of inspiration can be seen to be prefigured in the distinction Kierkegaard made between Christendom, the prevailing de-spiritualized Christianity as an institutional entity in a given historical period – and Christianity, the original spirit of the gospels in which the individual stands, in the inwardness of faith, in immediate, 'contemporaneous' relation to Christ irrespective of later developments in church history.

In our own time the movement toward the core commonality and renewed dialogue among religions is again being eclipsed and politically usurped. The term jihad which has been misappropriated by a small radical minority of Muslims to mean struggle against the enemies of Islam has been uncritically assumed and repeated by mainstream Western media and political figures. Its actual meaning in the Quran – 'the inward struggle' to live in the way of God – has been overlooked in the ensuing undifferentiated reaction, one that is taking on ominous dimensions, including the burning of the Quran.

In light of this hermetically sealed ideological echo chamber, Gallop's chairman and CEO, Jim Clifton, embarked on a six-year survey in thirty-five Muslim countries to determine what 1.3 billion Muslims actually thought about 9-11 and subsequent terrorist attacks. The results, collated by professor John Esposito of Georgetown University, show the great majority of Muslims unequivocally condemned the attacks. The recent opposition to a mosque in the vicinity of Ground Zero is in large part a case of displaced anger. One may also question the knowledge of those opponents of the work environment in the Twin Towers, for many critics are unaware of the mosque that already existed on the seventeenth floor of the South Tower – which was obliterated in the attack along with the Muslims who prayed there.

In a distant part of the world, on the Greek Island of Rhodes in the Aegean Sea, just southwest of Turkey, one will find, as in the mosque controversy about Ground Zero, an irrational animosity between Christians and Muslims that lingers to this day. One will encounter townspeople there who will pretend not to know the location of Suleiman Mosque. A persistent residue of bitterness of battles of past centuries can be detected owing to its location: it is built upon the ruins of the old Church of the Apostles. A local 'Christian' passerby may even be aggrieved were a visiting Christian to enter the mosque and wash his feet in the basin of the fountain amidst the platano trees in the triangular court. One may hear the reproof that a 'Christian church once stood here' – though in essence this comment, like the embittered debate over erecting a mosque at Ground Zero, deflects from the depth-dimension of both Christianity and Islam. For it is not the visible loci in space and time that are decisive, but the intimate I-Thou encounter and inwardness of prayer. In Matthew it reads, 'When you pray, go into your room, close the door, and pray to your Father, who is unseen' (6:6) So, too, may the Muslim be reminded of the same message in the Quran, 'Call on your Lord humbly and in secret.' (7:55)

A pivotal motivation for St. Francis in founding his order was to find modalities through which the focus on inner experience over the prevailing emphasis on external form and scholastic doctrinal argument could be transmitted in the Christian message. This inner experience is audible in the poem/song Cantico del Sol, Song of the Sun, composed while ministering to the poor and sick in his wanderings just after his visit to the East where Rumi in Damascus enlightened with lyrical insight and invoked the Deity with the devout dance of the whirling dervishes in semblance to the movement of celestial creation itself. The similarity of the verse of Francis with Rumi's poems Collection of the Sun of Tabriz, which were also sung, is striking. The contextual essence, symbols, and style that resonate from Rumi's incantations to those of Francis evince a deep affinity between these spiritual visionaries and the faiths they imbue to this day. In 2005 UNESCO declared the whirling dervish dance, otherwise known as The Mevevil Sema Ceremony, founded by the followers of Rumi, to be among the 'Masterpieces of the Oral and Intangible Heritage of Humanity.'

It is significant here that the Syrian educated Franciscan prodigy Roger Bacon, who founded the scientific method in the thirteenth century, posited the priority of experience in contrast to ecclesiastical overlay. The liberating implications of this distinction in the following centuries have been immense. In deference to his debt to the East, Bacon lectured at Oxford in Arab attire. Indeed, the attire of St. Francis of Assisi himself was that of the Sufi Muslims of Morocco and Spain – hooded cloak and wide sleeves.

In the night sky over the East and the West we need only look to the moon where a crater is named after the eleventh-century Persian polymath prodigy Avicenna in tribute to his studies in astronomy, which were far ahead of his time. This is a befitting symbol: with the first moon landing a shift in perspective was enacted: For the first time in history man can actually see earth as one unified entity.

We may also think of Avicenna as we enter the medical centers of the West. It is little realized that Avicenna, 'the prince of physicians', was the first to trace the transmission of disease by soil and water, and to note that tuberculosis is contagious, which was denied for centuries by European medicine. He shed light on the mind/body relation; and was the first to identify the frontal cortex of the brain as the locus of reasoning. His eminently enduring five volume Canon of Medicine is still taught at Yale and UCLA, among other medical schools in the West.

Yet in the theatre of religious discord prejudices proliferate like tainted microorganisms in a petri dish. When they resurfaced in our time in an uninformed, ethnocentric reading of cultures and religions entitled The Clash of Civilizations by Samuel Huntington of the Enterprise Institute it too was insightfully refuted, now by the multicultural Iranian-and German-educated Muslim scholar Mohammed Khatami in his edifying Dialogue of Civilizations. Khatami, when head of Iran's National Library, had infused it with the philosophical classics and scientific research of the West that he brought to bear in his reply. It so resonated with the international community that the UN named a resolution after its concept and proclaimed 2001, the year of its publication, the 'Year of Dialogue Among Civilizations.'

The priority of inner experience over dogma further resonates in Rumi's observation, 'A donkey loaded with holy books is still a donkey' and Francis's point, as related by Thomas of Celano, 'A great cleric must in some

The 15th century painting of St. Francis with Al Kamil in the courtyard believed to
be painted by Benozzo Gozzoli (In Public Domain)
(Scene 10, North Wall), 1452, Fresco,
270 x 220cm,
Apsidal chapel, San Francisco, Montefalco

Rumi by Lisa Dietrich,
Mixed media
9 x 10cm

way give up even his learning when he comes to the order.' This critique of doctrinal argument was central to the thought of the eleventh-century Jewish poet and philosopher Solomon Ibn Gabirol, known to the Muslims as Sulelman Ibn Yahya Jabriol, and to the Christians as Avicebron. His expansive perspective permeates the writings of those Jews, Christians and Muslims alike who were searching for the common origin of religious experience. Indeed, the major early Franciscan writers – Alexander of Hales, St. Bonaventure, Roger Bacon, and Duns Scotus – are all indebted to Ben Gabirol's Fons Vitae, Source of Life, which, in turn, was profoundly influenced by the Sufi Muslim thinker Muhammad Ibn Masarra. The Hebraic tradition has also thereby been enduringly enriched: Ibn Gabirol's main liturgical work Adon Olam is still chanted in synagogues; and his poetry sung in the Yom Kippur liturgy.

The eclipsed tapestry of this formative interfaith influence reappears in the twentieth century and beyond in the writings of one of the most important Catholic thinkers, the Trappist monk Thomas Merton. In a letter to the Pakistani scholar Abdul Aziz Merton writes, 'I am tremendously impressed with the solidity and intellectual sureness of Sufism ... There is no question but that here is a living and convincing truth, a deep mystical experience of the mystery of God our Creator.' Merton professed to Aziz a 'deep sympathy for Sufism,' for it is 'profoundly religious and set in the right perspective of direct relationship with the All-Holy God.'

To sever and parcel this spiritual tapestry is to sacrifice its essence. It would be as improvident in execution as unraveling the design of the Mihrab on a prayer rug, or picking apart the blue, purple, and scarlet threads of the Hebrew hoshen. The historical matrix it represents may be called a hologram of the holy. I borrow the term hologram from physics: an image, which when illuminated by a laser beam, has the appearance of being suspended in three-dimensional space. Any part of it, when provided with coherent light, provides an image of the entire Gestalt. We are reminded too of the net of Indra in Buddhist and Hindu mythology where each pearl reciprocally reflects the other, shedding light on the whole.

We are in need of an interfaith awakening, an epiphany of the order described by the Christian Tolstoy in the closing chapters of *Anna Karenina*. As Konstantin Levin stands on the terrace contemplating the constellations, he asks the question, What is the relationship to the Christian faith of the beliefs of the Jews, the Moslems, the Confucians, the Buddhists who also teach and do good? An analogy occurs to him. Much as we assume a sense of stability and preeminence on earth to trace the constellations, yet with the knowledge we are not at their centre but whirl in space as part of a larger universe we cannot fully comprehend, so too can we perceive the relative relation of religions to one another, while lacking an absolute perspective to judge their relation to the Deity.

George Tardios

Field-Weary

At root level
Grass sucks the sun green
Through its stem

The ram-Bull rises

Blown into shape
Out of mud
Swollen into prime cuts
Sodden with muscle

A heavy tart ballooning
On tittering stilettos.

Loaded genitals swing
Like billiard pouches,
A lead-head cosh,
An overloaded handbag

Full of liquid love
Winking at magpie coated cows
With one raw eye:

I am the Bull without
the horn
weary with loving
whole fields.

I am the Prologue Miller
with manners
my pilgrimage leads
to Aphrodite's shrine
always

my wish is to lie

Limp among dribbling grass
and become green –
deeply green –
all over.

Jeffrey Meyers

The Creative Moment Part One: Keats and Rimbaud

We are perennially fascinated by how poets transcend their early work, fulfill their potential and create great art. John Keats, Arthur Rimbaud, Wilfred Owen and Sylvia Plath afford precious insights into the mysteries of creativity. This essay will explore the lives of the first two poets and the other two will follow in the next issue. Isolated and lonely, a prey to melancholy and tormenting self-analysis, these doomed outsiders were driven by emotional turbulence, obsessed by morbid details and felt the need to suffer. All were threatened by imminent death and wrote with a desperate urgency; they knew they didn't have much time left and died young. Keats died from tuberculosis; Rimbaud from a self-destructive retreat from civilization that ended with syphilis, cancer and the amputation of his leg; Owen from enemy fire in war; Plath from suicide. But intense pressure can sometimes be inspiring. As Samuel Johnson observed, 'when a man knows he is to be hanged, it concentrates his mind wonderfully.' This morbid knowledge focused their minds and helped transform their feelings and ideas into poetry. Writing made it possible, suddenly and briefly, to conquer their psychological wounds. Cut off in their prime, they published very little in their lifetimes. Their tragic deaths enhanced their literary reputations and they received much greater posthumous recognition.

Keats (1795-1821)

Keats reached the height of his poetic genius and composed his five great odes – 'To Psyche,' 'On Indolence,' 'On a Grecian Urn,' 'To a Nightingale' and 'On Melancholy' – at the age of twenty-three in May 1819. The previous month, a typical quatrain in his 'La Belle Dame sans Merci' contained archaisms, banalities and clichés:

> She took me to her elfin grot,
>   And there she wept and sigh'd full sore,
> And there I shut her wild wild eyes
>   With kisses four.

He had been working on the long, unfinished 'Hyperion' and the short, tightly constructed sonnets, but abandoned them to concentrate on the more expansive lyric form of the odes.

Three biographical elements influenced Keats's change of mood, spurt of energy and natural flow of words. In June 1818 his younger brother, George, emigrated to America. He wrote that 'George always stood between me and any dealings with the world. Now I find I must buffet it – I must take my stand upon some vantage ground and begin to fight – I must choose between despair & Energy – I choose the latter.' Without George's financial and emotional support he was weaker and more vulnerable, but his brother's absence also stimulated him to be more self-sufficient. In long letters to George he defined his important ideas, sense of identity and source of poetic inspiration. Keats felt 'the World is full of Misery and Heartbreak, Pain, Sickness and Oppression,' but thought there must be some reason for all this suffering and tried to understand why he in particular had to suffer. He believed that pain disciplined his mind and created his personal identity as a poet. In April 1819 he wrote George, 'there may be intelligences or sparks of the divinity in millions – but they are not Souls till they acquire identities, till each one is personally itself.'

Keats had a great deal to sadden him. After George's departure he nursed his youngest brother, Tom, who died of tuberculosis in December 1818. Aileen Ward described how 'Keats returned to his long watch by Tom's bedside, nursing him through chills and coughing fits, trying to calm him in spells of despair, reading to him in his comfortable hours, and keeping up as cheerful a front as he could .... The hourly contact with his dying brother forced on him a new and painful self-awareness and with it a still more painful sense of self-division' from his apparent identity and his true self. Keats probably contracted the disease from his brother, whose tragic fate foreshadowed his own. He was constantly threatened by the sure and certain knowledge that he would also be destroyed by consumption. This gave him the morbid, premature feeling of 'the cold earth upon him' well before his own death in Rome at the age of twenty-five.

Keats's long expected and near fatal hemorrhage took place in February 1820, only nine months after he composed the great odes. With dramatic objectivity, he told Fanny Brawne, the girl he loved, 'On the night I was taken ill when so violent a rush of blood came to my Lungs that I felt nearly suffocated – I assure you I felt it possible I might not survive and at that moment thought of nothing but you.' Recalling his medical training, he added, 'I know the colour of that blood – it is arterial blood – I cannot be deceived in that colour; that drop is my death warrant. I must die.' In September 1820, just before his voyage to the warmer climate of Italy, he anticipated death as a relief from suffering while desperately clinging to the remnants of life: 'I wish for death every day and night to deliver me from these pains, and then I wish death away, for death would destroy even those pains which are better than nothing. Land and Sea, weakness and decline are great separators, but death is the great divorcer for ever.' Pain was better than nothing because it made him feel alive.

Keats's ineluctable fate both prevented his marriage to Fanny Brawne and made him eager to seize her love before it was too late. In May 1819 the teenaged Fanny was living with her family in the house next door to him in Wentworth Place (now Keats Grove) and he sometimes walked with her on Hampstead Heath. He idealized the beauty and wit of the rather shallow and self-absorbed girl, whom he called 'silly, fashionable and strange.' But that month he broke through the emotional barrier that had separated them and declared, 'I never knew before, such a love as you have made me feel.' Fanny was, undoubtedly, an attractive and inspiring presence.

Aware that he had reached a creative turning point, Keats told George that his 'Ode to Psyche' (and the odes that followed it) 'is the first and the only one with which I have taken even moderate pains – I have for the most part dash'd off my lines in a hurry – This I have done leisurely – I think it reads the more richly for it and will I hope encourage me to write other things in even a more peaceable and healthy spirit.' He also said, while trying to combine careful thought with the sudden rush of imaginative power, 'if Poetry comes not as naturally as the Leaves to a tree it had better not come at all.' His new spring of poetry did come naturally that month, with a personal urgency and mysterious release of energy that miraculously transformed his deepest feelings into words. He reached aesthetic maturity through an intense exploration of himself; achieved a heightened intensity of emotion, thought and act; and was exalted when, with full-throated ease, he felt possessed by his daemons and truly inspired. His friend Charles Brown left a vivid account of how Keats composed 'Ode to a Nightingale,' his supreme artistic achievement: 'In the spring of 1819 a nightingale had built her nest near my house. Keats felt a tranquil and continual joy in her song; and one morning he took his chair from the breakfast-table to the grass-plot under a plum-tree, where he sat for two or three hours. When he came into the house, I perceived he had some scraps of paper in his hand, and these he was quietly thrusting behind the books. On inquiry, I found those scraps, four or five in number, contained his poetic feeling on the song of our nightingale.'

Aileen Ward explained how the personal and poetic elements, especially his love for Fanny Brawne, coalesced into the long-awaited moment: 'For these few weeks he stood at a point of perfect balance, confident in his ability to meet the future, able to contemplate the past with calm, and rejoicing in the beauty of the season, the joy of an answered love, the delight of a mastered craft – the themes of the odes as well as his incentives to writing them.' But Walter Jackson Bate, emphasizing the darker aspects, described how Keats's fearful experience with death also permeated the poem: 'The personal poignance is obvious enough: Keats's constant exposure to death since the age of eight; the accumulated fatigue of the effort of the past four years; his uneasy feeling about his own future since he returned from Scotland with the "haunting sore-throat." Add to all this his attempts to manage this inevitable preoccupation with death.'

As Keats transforms the living bird into a symbol of visionary art, the nightingale's sweet song, like the poet's lyrical voice, stands out bravely against the suffering of the world. The ode expresses his awareness of joy and sadness, pleasure and pain as inseparable aspects of human life. He portrays a state of intense aesthetic and imaginative feeling, the conflict between momentary sensation and permanent art, and identifies with the natural song that exists beyond the world of change. Keats begins by stressing his physical weakness and psychological depression – 'My heart aches and a drowsy numbness pains / My sense,' where even intense pleasure can cause pain, and moves steadily, through a series of morbid images, toward death. He seeks escape from pain through drugs and wine, and hopes to fade into the nightingale's gentler world where time can no longer destroy youth and beauty. In a moving allusion to the death of young Tom and to the leaden coins that are placed on the eyes of the dead, he writes:

> Fade far away, dissolve, and quite forget
> What thou among the leaves hast never known,
> The weariness, the fever, and the fret
> Here, where men sit and hear each other groan;
> Where palsy shakes a few, sad, last gray hairs,
> Where youth grows pale, and specter-thin and dies;
> Where but to think is to be full of sorrow
> And leaden-eyed despairs,
> Where Beauty cannot keep her lustrous eyes,
> Or new Love pine at them beyond to-morrow.

In the sixth stanza Keats finally confronts death, which becomes a kind of spiritual transcendence and symbol of desirable fulfillment that allows him to escape from the human world of infinite suffering:

> Darkling I listen; and for many a time
> I have been half in love with easeful Death,
> Called him soft names in many a muséd rhyme,
> To take into the air my quiet breath;
> Now more than ever seems it rich to die,
> To cease upon the midnight with no pain,

While thou art pouring forth thy soul abroad
In such an ecstasy!
Still wouldst thou sing, and I have ears in vain –
To thy high requiem become a sod.

The poem ends with a melancholy awakening as Keats realizes that his poetical fancy can briefly propel him into the nightingale's world, but cannot sustain him there. His heightened imagination transcends reality, but he must inevitably feel pain when the spell is broken: 'Adieu! The fancy cannot cheat so well / As she is fam'd to do … Was it a vision, or a waking dream? / Fled is that music: – Do I wake or sleep?' Bate asserts that Keats's 'productivity of the three and a half weeks … is difficult to parallel in the career of any modern writer.' But there is, in fact, a similar surge of creative genius in the poetry of Rimbaud, Owen and Plath.

Rimbaud (1854-91)

Arthur Rimbaud's sophistication, poetic talent and extraordinary ideas exemplify the mystery of genius. In a notorious and influential letter of May 15, 1871 to his publisher-friend Paul Demeny, the sixteen-year-old provincial high-school dropout boldly defined his vision that demanded an artificially induced, self-destructive and deliberate derangement that would enable the tormented, sacrificial, even insane artist to become a great creator:

> The Poet makes himself a seer by a long, gigantic and rational derangement of all the senses. All forms of love, suffering, and madness. He searches himself. He exhausts all poisons in himself and keeps only their quintessences. Unspeakable torture where he needs all his faith, all his superhuman strength, where he becomes among all men the great patient, the great criminal, the one accursed – and the supreme Scholar! – Because he reaches the unknown! Since he cultivated his soul, rich already, more than any man! He reaches the unknown, and when, bewildered, he ends by losing the intelligence of his visions, he has seen them. Let him die as he leaps through unheard of and unnamable things.

Rimbaud's decision to derange the senses, including the most basic human emotions, seems willful and pathological, but was also rational and deliberate. He would take drink, drugs, even poison; he would endure unspeakable tortures, commit acts of violence, become a criminal, risk losing his poetic insights, even risk death. During his years with Paul Verlaine, Rimbaud put this mad programme into practice and, in the most intense emotional experience of his life, sucked the eager Verlaine into his whirlpool of depravity. But Verlaine didn't have to derange his senses to keep up with Rimbaud; he was already quite deranged when they first met.

As the younger Rimbaud dominated the weak-willed and besotted Verlaine, he experienced poverty and rebellion, starvation and exhaustion, filth and debauchery, degradation and disease, violence and destruction, while heightening his chaotic state with hashish and absinthe. The visionary yet analytic poet, determined to grasp the unknown, joyfully ruined himself in order to escape from ordinary life, enter a higher reality and gain superhuman poetical power. He survived by cultivating a spirit of revolt, and by pouring his anger and disgust into poetry.

Rimbaud began his torturous three year relationship with Paul Verlaine – poetic mentor, parent-substitute and lover – in 1871. Bored and penniless, he wrote to Verlaine, enclosing some of his poems. Instantly convinced of his genius, Verlaine invited him to leave home and live with him in Paris. Verlaine offered him exactly what he wanted: sufficient money, complete freedom, stimulating talk, artistic recognition, meetings with leading poets and useful contacts with editors. The critic W. H. Frohock called Rimbaud a deliberately boorish and disgusting 'juvenile delinquent with deviated tastes and possibly homicidal tendencies …. He was openly and aggressively offensive even to the associates who had befriended him. He lived parasitically on his friends, absorbed as much absinthe as he could, experimented with narcotics, tried to knife his companion, paraded his homosexuality, and broke up Verlaine's marriage.' He was at once chummy and caustic, flattering and sadistic, dominant and degraded, exalted and depraved, faithful and treacherous, angelic and demonic, radiant and disgusting, tender and violent, sexy and revolting, inspiring and cruel.

The tumultuous relationship of Rimbaud and Verlaine, the first open and defiant gay couple in literary history, ended in July 1873 when Verlaine shot Rimbaud and was sent to prison for two years. But the shooting incident in Brussels was more operatic than tragic. One bullet hit Rimbaud in the wrist, the other went into the wall of their hotel room. On hearing the shots Verlaine's mother, anxiously on guard next door, clumsily tried to help Rimbaud, whose wrist was bleeding profusely. Dazed and out of control, Verlaine sobbed on the bed, recovered slightly, gave Rimbaud the revolver and told him to 'unload it in my temple.'

Rimbaud's escape from his domineering mother and from his dull and stupefying home town, Charleville in northeast France, his rebellion against fashionable Parisian poets, sado-masochistic friendship with Verlaine (where poetry was the most important thing after sex and drink), and restless travels to Belgium and England catalyzed his volcanic outburst of brilliant poetry. Thomas Chatterton and Raymond Radiguet had much shorter lives, but were not as talented as Rimbaud. The lives of Keats, Owen and Plath were cut short, but they did not reach Rimbaud's impressive achievement while still in their teens. In one monstrous and miraculous year, from July 1872 to August 1873, Rimbaud wrote *Illuminations* and *A Season in Hell*. He began the latter in April 1873, while he was still entangled with Verlaine, and finished it in August, the month after he left him. His biographer Enid Starkie wrote that in the prose poem, 'the form best suited to his elliptical and hermetic style ... Rimbaud reached the highest peak of originality.'

Rimbaud's assertion that he's 'ripe for death' and attempt to escape from human suffering recall the major themes of Keats. *A Season in Hell* also has the long rhapsodic lines and emotional sweep of Walt Whitman's *Leaves of Grass*, the megalomaniacal iconoclasm of Friedrich Nietzsche's *Thus Spake Zarathustra* (Rimbaud also rejects morality as a 'weakness of the brain') and powerful affinities with Lautréamont's *Chants of Maldoror*. Like Rimbaud, Lautréamont led a wretched existence, died miserably (at the age of twenty-three) and achieved posthumous fame. Both writers were determined to reject normal life and fulfill their own creative destiny. Both poems – rapturous, hallucinatory, satanic monologues – resemble the musings of a maniac and revel in the most repulsive and self-immolating behavior. One critic's description of the *Chants of Maldoror* applies equally to *A Season in Hell:* 'an amazing profusion of apostrophe and imagery, at once delirious, erotic, blasphemous, grandiose and horrific.'

Rimbaud's confession and exorcism of a madman in hell – 'I think I am in hell, and therefore I am' – give a perverse twist to Descartes's *Cogito ergo sum*, and echo Christopher Marlowe's 'Why this is hell, nor am I out of it' in *Doctor Faustus* and John Milton's 'Which way I fly is hell; myself am hell' in *Paradise Lost*. The poem expands the ideas in Rimbaud's letter about the deliberate derangement of the senses as he 'plays clever tricks on insanity,' becomes the 'master of hallucinations' and looks on 'the disorder of [his] mind as sacred.' Wallowing in rage, debauchery and madness, he defiantly declares 'I have no moral sense. I am a brute … a beast, a savage … burdened with vice that sank its roots of suffering at my side as early as the age of reason – and that rises to the sky, batters me, knocks me down, drags me after it.' Declaring, 'I am an outcast. I loathe my country,' he predicts with amazing accuracy, 'I am leaving Europe. The sea air will burn my lungs. Lost climates will tan me. I will swim, trample the grass, and smoke. I will drink alcohol as strong as boiling metal' and wander to the ends of the earth.

A Season in Hell, especially the section called 'Delirium' where Rimbaud portrays Verlaine as 'The Foolish Virgin' and himself as 'The Infernal Bridegroom,' parodies their homosexual life together as an unreal and perverse form of marriage. He misleadingly characterizes himself as passive and innocent, and portrays Verlaine as the pathetic slave of the demon lover who torments and finally abandons him. In the poem the older poet says:

> He was almost a child …. His mysteriously delicate feelings had seduced me. I forgot all my human duty to follow him. What a life! Real life is absent. We are not in the world. I go where he goes. I have to. And often he flies into a rage at me, poor me. The Demon! He is a demon, you know. He is not a man …. Then he

would recover his manners of a young mother, of an older sister. If he were less wild, he would be saved! But his tenderness too is mortal. I am a slave to him. – Oh! I am mad! …

We worked together in a state of joy. But after a penetrating caress, he would say: 'It will seem strange to you, when I am not here any more – after all you have gone through. When you will no longer have my arms under your neck, and my heart to lay your head on, and my lips on your eyes. Because one day I will have to go off, very far off.

Rimbaud's 'late work' was written in his late teens. He wrote his best poetry during his most turbulent times with Verlaine, and gave up writing just after their violent quarrel and final separation. Consistently perverse, Rimbaud renounced poetry at the age of twenty and at the height of his powers, and finished up with an Abyssinian mistress, a cancerous amputated leg and a prosthetic limb that didn't work. His poems, like the powerful beacon of a lighthouse, briefly lit up the landscape before disappearing into the dark.

Edward Lucie-Smith

Object Lessons

I'm a relentless accumulator of objects – in other words an impassioned collector, quite unable to restrain myself from acquiring new items – to the damage of my bank account, and even if I no longer have room to show them off to advantage. These objects tend to be old, often very ancient indeed, rather than being contemporary. This, despite the fact that I write very frequently about the excitements and vagaries of contemporary art.

This preference is rooted, not in one place, but in several. For example, the brutal truth is that nowadays it is usually much cheaper to buy an extremely ancient item than it is to buy one of equivalent quality from our own day. Add to this the fact that many of these ancient objects often seem both more radical and more imaginative than the supposedly avant-garde products of our own time. Add to this, again, the resonances that these items have, simply because of their age, and what they seem to tell one about how both social and aesthetic attitudes have and haven't changed in the course of many centuries.

My approach, however, is even more atavistic than this. I was born and grew up in Jamaica. Whatever, its other attractions – the surrounding sea, the broad beaches, the sumptuous wildness of tropical nature in many parts of the island's mountainous interior – it is not a place that has much to offer to a lover of museums. The Spaniards, the first European possessors of the place, more or less wiped out the indigenous inhabitants – Native American Tainos, who had migrated there from the mainland of South and Central America. Reporting to his royal patrons in Spain about indigenous people from the same stock encountered in the Bahamas, Columbus said:

> These people have little knowledge of fighting, as Your Majesties
> will see from the seven I have captured to take away with us so
> as to teach them our language and return them, unless your Maj-

esties' orders are that they all be taken to Spain or held captive on the island itself, for with fifty men one could keep the whole population in subjection and make them do whatever one wanted.

The Taino of Jamaica had no resistance to the new diseases the conquerors brought with them. They took sick, they died, and they vanished from recorded history.

The truth is that before its capture in 1655 from its Spanish garrison by a British expedition commanded by Robert Venables and William Penn, Jamaica's past is more or less a blank. The British conquest was a consolation prize for a failed attack in Hispaniola. The Commonwealth government was so displeased by the result that both commanders were imprisoned on their return. Most of the troops they left behind them sickened and died, as the Taino had done before them. It was only after some decades, and the import of numerous enslaved Africans via the Middle Passage, that sugar-producing Jamaica became a hugely valuable possession.

If there were no museums worthy of the name in Kingston there was at least a good library at the Institute of Jamaica. From an early age I was an avid reader, often of books one wouldn't have expected to attract some one still in his early teens. It was there that I discovered and devoured Howard Carter's three-volume account of his discovery and excavation of the tomb of Tutankhamen, which fired my enthusiasm for this long ago ancient civilization. At night I used to lie in bed, imagining I had been allowed to visit the courtyard of a marvellous eighteenth-Dynasty palace, complete with sphinxes and a pool.

When I came to live in London, immediately following the war, there was another piece of happenstance. At the far end of Sydney Street in Chelsea where my mother bought a house, there was a little, ramshackle shop, now long demolished. These were the premises occupied by K. J. Hewett. A paragraph on the website of the British Museum describes him as having 'had a major influence on collectors of antiquities and ethnographic arte-facts from the 1950s to the 1980s'. I was soon running in and out, running errands, being allowed to handle items from his stock. From time to time I made a small purchase out of my pocket money. I remember a Roman bronze of a cormorant, which cost, I think, fifteen pounds – quite a large sum for me at the time.

The shop was a gathering place for a group, mostly much senior to myself, whom I now think of as the devotees of André Malraux's newly invented musée imaginaire. Sir Robert and Lady Sainsbury visited. So did the sculptor Jacob Epstein. Much closer to me in age was George Ortiz, the grandson of the Bolivian tin king, Simón Iturri Patiño. George, short of stature and wonderfully impassioned by nature, was known to amused friends as 'Mighty Mouse'. He hated hotels, and for a period, when I moved into the upper maisonette of the house still occupied by my mother, he took over my miniscule spare bedroom for his frequent visits to London. He was then busy building up the finest private collection of Greek, Roman and Ancient Egyptian objects to be formed in my lifetime. Some items roosted for a while amid the sheets and bathroom towels in my linen cupboard.

The idea of a musée imaginaire, of course, was largely the result of the new possibilities been offered by the art book publishing industry, as it revived after the war. Big illustrated books, with lots of colour, became easier and easier to produce. The expanded consciousness of the huge variety of different cultures that had existed or still existed in the world was the product of this, while art books, in turn, spread the word about kinds of art, and especially the ancient and ethnographic varieties of art, which until then had remained comparatively inaccessible. So too did increasing ease of travel.

These developments, however, were not free of a subtle taint of colonialism. The assumption was that the truly refined western aesthete would always be capable of discerning what was and wasn't a masterpiece, even if he (or she) knew next to nothing about the culture that had produced it.

Essentially this was not only the beginning of my voyage as a collector, but the start of the circuitous route that has brought me to where I now am, which has involved some drastic changes of attitude. Objects have come and gone, according to the state of my finances at the time. Some I bitterly regret having being forced to part with, but not many, there is always the pleasure of beginning again. Beginning afresh, I no longer believe one can get much from works of art while maintaining a willed ignorance of their cultural, social and historical context.

The object I have chosen to discuss here is something I wouldn't have looked at with much interest in the old days. Now, for the moment at least, it fascinates me, for reasons that are no longer purely aesthetic. It is a life-size terracotta head of a Sogdian merchant or mercenary soldier, a forceful, almost caricatured, portrait of a recognizable individual if ever there was one. If you met him in the flesh, and you'd previously seen this head, you'd know him at once.

When I use the word 'Sogdian' I immediately seem to hear a murmur of 'what?' or 'who?' Sogdians are one of those lost peoples, who, like the Taino, have almost disappeared from the historical record. They were Eastern Iranians, who came from the Central Asian region around Bukhara and Samarkand. Originally Zoroastrians, many later became Buddhists, and eventually made the transition to Islam. At the time that concerns me now, that of the Tang, the greatest of all Chinese dynasties, they were the facilitators who ran the Silk Route, which joined East to West, overland.

There are many images of Sogdians to be found among the terracotta and (later on) glazed ceramic figures with which the Chinese elite of the Han and Tang dynasties filled their tombs. Called mingqi —'spirit utensils' — these aimed to provide the deceased with all the comforts and entertainments they had enjoyed while alive. In addition to human figures there are many representations of animals, both familiar and mythical. The mythical ones served as guardians to protect the tomb.

There are also miniature ceramic version of tools and domestic items, such as ovens. In some cases the tomb would be provided with an entire farm, complete with all the appropriate structures – a house for the farmer, plus granaries, watchtowers, even a well.

Life-size terracotta head of a Sogdian (Eastern Iranian) soldier or merchant, Chinese, Tang Dynasty, 618-907

The tomb figures of this period are never life-size. The very largest, such as some examples in the collection of the British Museum, are about a metre high. The makers of these ceramic sculptors seem to have taken a particular delight in making images of non-Chinese ethnic types, which tend to be much more vividly characterized than their native Chinese counterparts.

The Sogdians portrayed in these statuettes fall into several fairly tightly restricted categories. There are entertainers – musicians and dancers. Sometimes one finds a whole band, equipped with a conductor, waving his arms, often covered in long flowing sleeves, to keep time for the other members of his orchestra. There are merchants and their employees – camel drivers and grooms. There are soldiers, often mounted. I had never, until I came across the sculpture illustrated here, encountered a life-sized portrait of a Sogdian, unmistakably from this ethnic group both because of his distinctively non-Chinese facial features, and also because of the turban-like hat or cap that he wears. This distinctive headdress is can be found on all the small figures of musicians, merchants, grooms and soldiers that I have just cited.

Life-sized heads do occasionally occur amongst Chinese Han and Tang terracottas, but these are invariably bland heads of the Buddha, related to images that one also finds as carvings in stone. Where representations of individual human beings are concerned the Chinese, almost throughout what we now think of as 'dynastic' times, never seem to have been much interested in creating specific individualized human likenesses in three dimensions. The major exceptions to this are the life-size figures of the celebrated 'Terracotta Army', made for the vast mausoleum of Qin Shi Huang, the so-called First Emperor of China, who reigned in the third-century BC, We know the figures were made on an assembly line principle, heads, arms, legs and torsos being molded separately, then put together, and we also know that only about eight standard face moulds were used. It was clever tweaking or these archetypes that allowed the assembly line craftsmen to create images that often seem incredibly individual. However this happened nearly a millennium before my head of a Sogdian was probably made. Nobody who followed the First Emperor was able to afford quite such a lavish tomb complex, though later on the burial places of the great were often magnificent enough.

The point about my head of a Sogdian, however, is not simply its individuality – the fact that it brings vividly to life a person from a culture one can now scarcely imagine. It's also that, like the book I read in my early teens about Tutankhamen's tomb, it summons up a lost world and a dramatic story. It excites the imagination, not just the aesthetic sense. If it is in fact Tang, rather than Han (which it also might be) it offers a tenuous link to one of the greatest upheavals China ever experienced.

In the mid-eighth century CE China was at the height of its early prosperity, while Europe, after the collapse of the Roman Empire, was just emerging from what we now call the Dark Ages. It was not till 800 that Charlemagne became the first sovereign since the Roman collapse to rule over all of what had once been the Western territories of the Empire. He was crowned in the old St Peter's Basilica in Rome on Christmas Day of that year.

The Tang government held a census in 754. It showed that the Tang realm contained 1,859 cities, 321 prefectures and 1,538 counties. There are wildly varying estimates of the total Chinese population at that time, ranging from around one hundred million to two hundred and forty million or more. The population of Western Europe had meanwhile been sinking for some centuries. An estimate made in 2010, by Paolo Malanima, a researcher at the Institute of Studies on Mediterranean Societies, suggests it was, by the middle of the eighth century, just fifty-six million.

The Tang Emperor Xuanzong, on the throne in mid-eighth century, had for some years skilfully held the various factions at his court in balance, but he was becoming tired of the business of ruling, and increasingly preoccupied with a lover, the beautiful Yang Kuei-Fei. She had been married to one of his sons, and he took her away from him and made her his chief concubine. She was exquisite, so the sources tell us, with a voluptuous figure (reflected in the 'court lady' minqi figurines often found in Tang tombs), and was celebrated in poems by the greatest poet of the age, Li Bai:

She is the flowering branch of the peony,
Richly-laden with honey-dew.
Hers is the charm of the vanished fairy,
That broke the heart of the dreamer king
In the old legend of Cloud and Rain.

A problematic major personality at this time, sometimes present at Xuan-zong's court, sometimes guarding the frontiers, was the barbarian general An Lushan, who was partly of Sogdian and partly of Turkish stock. He was treated with great favour by the Emperor, and given a magnificent property in the bustling capital Chang'an. He was a huge man, enormously fat, also rough-mannered and illiterate, a complete contrast to the refined literati scholars, picked after a gruelling series of examinations, who now ran most aspects of the imperial administration. He amused Yang Kue-Fei, who formally adopted him, presenting his vast form to the court all wrapped up in swaddling clothes.

The ambitious general eventually fell out with Xuanzong's chief minister, who was also Yang Kue-Fei's cousin. In 755 he rebelled, proclaiming himself the head of a new dynasty. He took Luoyang, the second largest city in China, and moved on Chang'an. The Emperor and his entourage fled towards Chengdu in distant Sichuan. Their party didn't get very far. At a posting station just over thirty miles from the capital their escort mutinied, and demanded the deaths of both the chief minister and his relative the favourite. Yang Kuei-Fei was strangled with a silken cord, supplied by the Emperor himself. The date was July 15th 755, and she was then aged thirty-seven.

In later ages, she became a legendary figure, celebrated not only in China but also in Japan. Another Tang poet, Bai Juyi, from a later phase of the dynasty, wrote a famous lament for her, which carried her story down through the ages:

The emperor's green-canopied carriage
Was forced to halt,

Having left the west city gate
More than a hundred li.
There was nothing the emperor could do,
At the army's refusal to proceed.
So she with the moth-like eyebrows
Was killed before his horses.
Her floral-patterned gilded box
Fell to the ground, abandoned and unwanted,
Like her jade hair-pin
With the gold sparrow and green feathers
(Bai Juyi, Song of the Everlasting Sorrow)

An Lushan did not last long after he rebelled. He became increasingly paranoid and was assassinated by his son in 757. The rebellion, marked by more assassinations, lingered on until 763. The Tang Dynasty survived and did not finally collapse until 907, but was never the force it had once been. The revolt is said to have caused at least thirty-six million deaths. In proportion to the world's total population at that time, this was a larger percentage loss than that caused by either of the two twentieth-century World Wars.

When I now look at my portrait of a Sogdian many thoughts run through my mind. I think, for example, of the phenomenal recent rise, both economic and in terms of political power, of the China we know today. Its swarming metropolises, Beijing and Shanghai, seem like the contemporary equivalents of eighth-century Chang'an and Luoyang, both huge cities in their day. Chang'an had over two million inhabitants, Luoyang over a million. I also think of that undercurrent of mistrust of all foreigners, all non-ethnic Chinese, that one sometimes senses in China, however many Chinese friends one may personally have. People trace this to the negative impact made on Chinese society in the nineteenth-century by aggressive European colonialism, the burning of the Summer Palace in 1860 by British troops has still not been forgiven. A British captain in the Engineers, present at the sack, rightly described it as 'wretchedly demoralizing work for an army.'

In fact I think this mistrust may go much further back. Tang China was more fully open to the outside world, at least in the earlier, more glorious years of the dynasty, than it has ever been since. This is what my Sogdian merchant or soldier reminds me of. I wonder about the adventurous life he must have led, moving along the Silk Route. I wonder why some Chinese nobleman or magnate chose to welcome him to the eternal slumbers of his tomb.

Complement your subscription of The London Magazine with our

2014 Diary

and save 15% off the retail price

Subscribe today by completing our subscription form or simply visit:

thelondonmagazine.org

THE LONDON MAGAZINE

**Subscribe to the finest original short fiction and poetry,
exclusive essays and reviews in print and online six times a year**

Title _____ First name _____ Last name _____

Address _____

Town _____ Postcode _____

Country _____

Email _____

IF BUYING AS A GIFT PLEASE INDICATE RECIPIENT'S DETAILS BELOW:

Title _____ First name _____ Last name _____

Address _____

Town _____ Postcode _____

Country _____

Email _____

Subscription options (all prices are in £GBP and include postage):

One Year (6 Issues)

☐   United Kingdom £33   ☐ + Diary £43.15

☐   Europe Airmail £40   ☐ + Diary £53.40

☐   Rest of World Airmail £51   ☐ + Diary £64.40

Two Years (12 Issues)

☐   £59   ☐ + Diary £69.15

☐   £72   ☐ + Diary £85.40

☐   £92   ☐ + Diary £105.40

Payment method:

☐   I enclose a cheque/postal order/international money order for £_____ payable to 'The London Magazine'

☐   Please debit my credit/debit card for £_____ Cardholder name: _____

Card type (Visa/Master Card) number: _ _____ _____

Expiry date:_____/_____ Issue date:_____/_____ Issue number:_____ Security code:_____

Please send your subscription form to:
The London Magazine
11 Queens Gate
London
SW7 5EL

Tel: 020 7584 5977
thelondonmagazine.org

Sanjeev Sethi

Suffrage

My eyes are calloused with the curse
of not being able to get your glimpse.
My irises are templates of yearning.

I have decided to be in control –
like how the handbooks
expect of us when we seek oneness.

I will be earnest about my etiquettes.
Follow the grammar of successful regimes.
Please vote me in.

Mary O'Shea

Enclosed Orders

It was on page thirteen of *Le Figaro*, among items of national interest: an appeal by Monseigneur Jérôme Vallon on behalf of the Carmelite nuns of Nîmes for information relating to one of their community. After twenty-eight years of contemplative life, Soeur Agathe had disappeared. The order wanted to know that she was safe and well.

On the stairs, I pass Mme Perrault brandishing a polish-encrusted cloth and intent on delaying all comers. I engage without stopping: most of the concierges I know are mentally unhinged and ours is no exception.

Out in the bitter January morning, something between a wind and a gale, armed with invisible nails, is travelling down the street. I fix my scarf around my mouth and nose. I try to see what Soeur Agathe would see on her first day in the world after three decades of devotion to a higher cause. She shadows me on my usual route: past Sabbia Rosa's delectable lingerie, the antique map shop, the art boutiques, Cartier, Sonia Rykiel, the bookstores, the bars and restaurants made famous in the fifties. We arrive at the square where traffic is already building and exhaust fumes dance in the air. Women of our age and older, impeccable even in extremes of temperature, make their solitary way along the pavements.

She won't have shopped for a while so I take her on a tour of the food aisles in Monoprix on rue de Rennes. My life, as I choose my fruit and inhale the perfume of fresh bread, seems sweet. Already, in my head, a letter is composing itself:

Dear Soeur Agathe,

I have read about you in Le Figaro and I would like to invite you to Paris. Come for a week or a month. We will shop and

stroll and sit in the Café de Flore (a small extravagance), drink-
ing coffee and eating hard-boiled eggs with toasted brioche. We
will talk about your life, and about mine. I have hundreds of
books and an extensive music collection. I especially like jazz,
the bluesy kind. I can offer you a sofa bed which is really very
comfortable. The Sixth, where I live, is quiet and safe.

But quiet and safe is what she has just fled from, and hardly without deep and painful consideration. *It is noisy where I live, and increasingly danger-ous, but one gets used to it...?* No. It wouldn't do to begin with lies.

It's been a long time since anyone stayed with me. I fill the trolley with the usual things, adding a tub of tabbouleh, just to see. I wheel my purchases around to Dispatch, give my details for the afternoon delivery and take with me enough food for lunch. At the snack bar, I place my coat and scarf on a neighbouring stool and plan to defend it with the expected arrival of my imaginary friend, should anyone enquire. I order a *pain aux raisins* with an espresso. I don't usually take a pastry because I am not much given to physical exercise and so I have to be careful about what I eat.

How long before she tells me everything? I will, of course, want to know how she closed the door on twenty-eight years, and why. How long had she been preparing? Where did the seed come from that grew into a ladder of escape? Did it come by invitation or by accident? Or did she step, heed-lessly, through an open garden gate into the pale January street to be swept along on the hypnotic pulse of a town bent in perpetual adoration of slick, forgiving, more comfortable gods? And was she then unable to return?

'So,' she will turn her brand new eyes on me. 'Tell me about you.'

Where to start? Will I say that I was born into a household in the grip of rules and penalties and random affection? That my sister was five years younger and we were never friends? That the garden around the house boasted perfect lawns and flowerbeds and a lily pond where unwanted kit-tens met their end? That outside my bedroom window was a tree bearing apples the same heroic red as Maman's lipstick? Those apples clung to their branches up to the feasts of saints and spirits when most of the trees were bare. After falling, they lay a long time on the ground seemingly intact while the underside was devoured by fat, white maggots. My spine retains a memory of the shock I felt when I saw that. *Sometimes it's best –* Papa told me *– not to turn things over*. I will expect her to understand why I would not have questioned his wisdom.

As for the rest, she may not approve. But approval is, I think, generally overrated.

****

I wander back to the apartment. Mme Perrault pokes her head out as I cross the vestibule.

'Monsieur is already above,' she says reverently.

'Monsieur?'

It's Tuesday: I'm not expecting Bertrand. Her eyebrows rise at least two centimetres. (He gives her a box of chocolates at Christmas.)

'Ah, yes,' I say. 'Thank you, Madame.'

And indeed, there he is, seated on the blue brocade chair by the window where the light is good, folding *Le Figaro* as I enter.

'Why is your mobile turned off?' he says.

'It's in the bedroom, charging.'

'Why don't you charge it at night, like everyone else? I was on the point of leaving.'

'Did we have an arrangement for today?'

He comes over to where I'm standing and puts a pouting face against mine. The appearance of woe comes naturally to him.

'Bertrand, it's Tuesday.'

'But Estelle has gone to the country to spoil our son while his Sarah Bernhardt of a wife is in hospital. So, here I am, with you. Tell me you're overjoyed to see me.'

'How is the little drama queen?'

I should explain that a part of my life – too big a part – is lived in the anteroom of a family, behind a wall of one-way glass. I see them all, know them all, and only Bertrand sees me. Central Paris holds two million souls: once we are discreet, there is little danger of exposure. I know what the menopause is doing to Estelle and that she suffers from in-growing toenails. I know that their son Hugues was a child given to stealing from his mother's purse, and biting. I know things about Bertrand that only Estelle should know. Once or twice, I have suspected that behind yet another wall of one-way glass there may be another woman, younger perhaps and with a bolder gaze, who sees what I see but who also sees me.

'Ah! I'm sure it's nothing more than anxiety. Once the baby arrives, she'll have to pull herself together.' His expression softens. 'I can't believe it. You know, I look in the mirror and say to myself: Bertrand, you are too young to be a grandfather. And I am. I am too young, aren't I?'

More than a smile, a golden ray of anticipation illuminates his face: until this birth he has been only a husband and a father. I would have liked children of my own, a regular family, but the time has passed.

The baby, as we already know, is a girl. Her name will be Aude. Weekend visits will produce an endless stream of descriptions. On the flat, dull surface of my life he will construct images of her loveliness. There will be photographs, DVDs, anecdotes in abundance. I will never set my eyes on her but I will come to know her face, her endearing ways, as well as any mother. Hugues was sixteen when I met Bertrand but Aude will be new: she will inhabit by right our time together and I will be unable to keep her out.

'What did you bring?' He teases open the side of the shopping bag. 'Ham and olives – good. But what on earth is tabbouleh? What were you thinking, Marianne?'

'So, food is what you came for?' I say, swatting away his hand.

'You know you are my food, my nourishment.'

It amazes me that he can still say these things.

There is a link, of course, between sex and food. In the early stage of our relationship, sex was like a portion of foie gras: if it slipped off a plate in the kitchen to be accidentally trodden on by an over-worked sous-chef, it would still be delicious. With foie gras, what you get is seldom less than you expect. But, over time, sex comes to resemble foie gras less and onion soup more. Onion soup is a dish that can be spoilt by any one of a number of minor things: too much salt, too much bread (or the wrong sort), an excess or a shortage of liquid, poor quality cheese transformed into an impenetrable lid. At its best, it is the most satisfying food; at its worst, it is indigestible and potentially life-threatening.

He must, like me, be disappointed sometimes, bored by the routine, frustrated by the dead-end nature of it. But he never says. Our compensations have been modest: an occasional weekend in the country, a few days midweek in another city on the pretext of work. Time stolen from his company, intimacy stolen from his wife: the thief is Bertrand. And I? An accomplice, maybe, often the beneficiary, but not the primary guilty party. I no longer think too much about that aspect of it. I have had to accept that he means more to me than I to him, though I have no one to betray.

He kisses the sensitive spot on the nape of my neck. I would like to be strong but, when all is said and done, I too have my needs.

Almost an hour later we are becalmed, our limbs mingled in familiar disarray. It is that bittersweet moment between the glow of union and the chill of imminent separation.

'Did you read about the nun?' I ask.

'What nun?'

'In *Le Figaro*. She absconded from an enclosed order after twenty-eight years. Can you imagine?'

'I must have skipped over it.'

'They're appealing for information.'

'Alzheimer's,' he says. 'She'll be wandering around some shopping arcade.'

'She can't be much older than me.'

'Depression. They should be dragging the river.'

'Why?'

'Marianne! After half a lifetime of virtual imprisonment, there's no chance she'll survive out there.'

I have not considered such possibilities. I want to know where she is. Has she gone to a seaside town in the south or west, trading her limited skills? She will have no mobile phone, no computer literacy, no sense of how the world has changed in three decades. But she can garden, I'm sure, and sew and cook and clean. She may even know how to keep accounts. She is capable, certainly, of caring for the sick, of comforting the dying. She is patient and clever and keeps her counsel to herself. She is outstandingly brave. I think I have never admired anyone in quite the way I admire her.

'If I disappeared, Bertrand, would you look for me?'

'So, this is your plan?'

'Would you put a notice in the paper?'

'Sometimes, I suspect that you are just a little bit crazy. But I love you, even so.'

After a light salad accompanied by wine, it is time for him to leave. He stands in the doorway, his navy wool coat turned up at the collar. I rest my fingertips on the wiry hair below his temples and my thumbs smooth back the wild line of his brows.

'Bertrand, I have loved you too well.'

'Be honest, now. You don't do badly.'

'No, but my life doesn't really feel like my own.'

'Sweet Marianne! Love is love. You know there's no such thing as loving too well.'

And so he goes, descending the stairs while I lean over the banister and wait until he is in the vestibule where, when the coast is clear, he turns to blow me a kiss. Today, Mme Perrault is polishing; they exchange polite greetings but he does not look up. The click of the entrance door resounds in the gleaming hall.

The rooms to which I return are warm and airless. Often I lie on the bed after he leaves, aware of a hollow bud in my solar plexus attempting to unfurl. Today, I am restless and roam around. On our plates, each of us has left a mound of olive stones, his neater than mine. A shower of golden breadcrumbs is already hardening on the table. In the base of our glasses is a dark stain of wine. On the countertop, plastic salad tubs lie gaping beside shells of avocado pear.

Although I am not at all hungry, I open the tabbouleh and dip a fork in. The taste is pleasant: dry and spicy and sweet. I take it with me to the window, continuing to eat. Below, people are making their way muffled in scarves and overcoats. For a week, there has been talk of snow.

Seeing Bertrand without warning always unsettles me. Once – it was a Saturday morning, quite early, the sun powering up along the river and patterning the wooden planks of the Pont des Arts with a trellis of shadows – I saw him a little distance ahead, going in the direction of the right bank. I was on my way to La Samaritaine which, unfortunately, has since closed down. I smiled to myself, not thinking it was he but someone who resembled him. Getting closer, I saw that it was in fact Bertrand. A combination of shock and caution slowed me down. Early morning roller-bladers wound in and out between us, making the wooden boards rumble. I felt unsafe, as though I could easily be knocked over or lose my footing. I wanted him to turn round and see me. And then I wanted him not to. The idea of an earthquake came into my mind: the way bridges rear up and split and yawn apart. He would make it to the other bank while I would hit the water or tumble back to where I came from. He had no business that I knew of on my side of town.

I have made attempts to end it. 'This is not good for me, Bertrand,' I have said. 'We should part.' This would be a useful ploy if I were an acquisitive person, because such statements result in gifts, treats, renewed protestations of love and need, beside which a frail bid for freedom is easily thwarted. I am not resolute. I am too used to my security, too fond of my comforts.

She must, like me, have thought about leaving, and fought off thinking about it, until it came to occupy the whole space of her will. Even so, how did she steel herself to forsake the simple safety of her cell with its narrow bed and the crucifix overhead, the silent companionship of the refectory, the lullaby of litanies? She must have feared the lingering echo of hymns chanted by her sisters, glimpsed how the slow, lavish *Tantum Ergo* might disturb her serenity across unknown tracts of space and time. She must have wondered how long it would take for those familiar harmonies to fade.

But still, the day came when she folded her robes and her veil, when she slipped the ring from her finger, her dream of eternal salvation surrendered, the husband of her soul abandoned. The day came. It would not have come in a single rush. No, it would have approached her imperceptibly, with miniscule shifts in the weight of words, gestures, moments of labour and repose.

I would like to be sure, before I choose it, that freedom is what I want. But how can I be sure, when it has no colour, no resonance or scent, no sweetness, no tender touch? To choose without knowing is a hard thing, yet, I am afraid that if I wait until I am certain, it will already be too late. Even though there is a chance that freedom is not what I want, somehow, for me too, the time has come. I must be strong. I must be resolute, like her.

****

He will wonder where I have gone but he will place no advertisements to assure himself of my safety. He will not file a missing persons report. He will judge me to be callous, selfish, ungrateful. He will find consolation in the smile of his grandchild, in the laughter of family Sundays, in the simple joys. He will lean a little more on Estelle and keep an eye open over her shoulder for someone who reminds him in a particular way of me.

As for Soeur Agathe: I see her in my mind's eye on a tree-lined street far from her place of bondage, turning the key in her own front door. I see her mounting a narrow stairway, entering an apartment, setting down a bag of inexpensive food. There is a mirror where she checks the growth of her hair, where she notes again with some surprise the colour of her eyes, the true shape of her head and face, a mirror where she dares to cloud the glass with a whisper of her old, lost name. What could it be? Lorette? Mathilde? Geneviève?

It is winter there too. The weather is breathtakingly cold but the world is new, glinting with beauty and danger.

This story was awarded second place in *The London Magazine*'s Short Story Competition 2012 which was judged by Edna O'Brien, Alison MacLeod and Cathy Galvin.

Notes on Contributors

Peter Abbs is Emeritus Professor of Creative Writing at the University of Sussex. He is the author of a number of books on aesthetic education and eleven volumes of poetry. The most recent, *Voyaging Out,* was published by Salt in 2009. See www.peterabbs.org

Lana Asfour is a journalist based in London and Beirut. Her writing and photographs have appeared in a variety of publications. She completed her Ph.D. in Modern Languages and Literature at Oxford University, spending some time as a visiting researcher at the École Normale Supérieure in Paris and the American University of Beirut, and has taught at the Open University and Queen Mary-University of London. Her first book, *Laurence Sterne in France* (2008), was well reviewed by the Times Literary Supplement and other journals. She has been named one of *Granta's* 'New Voices.'

Norman Buller's verse has appeared widely in the UK and abroad. He has had five poetry collections published by Waterloo Press, the latest being *Pictures of the Fleeting World* (2012). His work can be accessed at www.normanbuller.me.uk.

Anne Chisholm is a biographer, and Chair of the Royal Society of Literature.

David Cooke won a Gregory Award in 1977 and published his first collection, *Brueghel's Dancers* in 1984. His retrospective collection, *In the Distance*, was published in 2011 by Night Publishing and a collection of more recent pieces, *Work Horses*, has just been published by Ward Wood Publishing. His poems, translations and reviews have appeared widely in journals including *Agenda, Ambit, The Bow Wow Shop, The Irish Press, The London Magazine, Magma, The North, Poetry Ireland Review, Poetry London, Poetry Salzburg Review, The Reader, The SHOP* and *Stand.*

Will Eaves is the author of three novels and one collection of poems. *The Absent Therapist*, a volume of experimental fiction, will be published by CB Editions early in 2014. He teaches at the University of Warwick.

Ruth Fainlight was born in New York City, but has lived in England since the age of fifteen. She has published thirteen collections of poems in England and the USA, as well as two volumes of short stories, and translations from several languages. Books of her poetry have appeared in French, Italian, Portuguese, Romanian and Spanish translation. She received the Hawthornden and Cholmondeley Awards in 1994, and is a Fellow of the Royal Society of Literature. Her collection *Sugar-Paper Blue* was short-listed for the 1998 Whitbread Award. Her *New & Collected Poems* was published in the UK by Bloodaxe Books in 2010.

Chrissie Gittins's collections are *Armature* (Arc) and *I'll Dress One Night As You* (Salt). Her pamphlet collection *Professor Heger's Daughter* will be published by Paekakariki Press, printed in traditional letterpress. Her three children's poetry collections are all Poetry Book Society Choices for the Children's Poetry Bookshelf and two were shortlisted for the CLPE Poetry Award. She has made an hour's recording for the Poetry Archive and her new and collected children's poems *Stars in Jars* will be published by Bloomsbury in February 2014. Chrissie also writes radio drama, and her short story collection is *Family Connections* (Salt). www.chrissiegittens.co.uk

Stuart Henson's most recent collection, *The Odin Stone*, is published by Shoestring Press.

Anthony Head is a senior editor at Kyodo News, Japan's main news agency, based in Tokyo. His articles have appeared in numerous journals, including *History Today, Prospect, Edinburgh Review* and the *TLS*. He is the editor of three volumes of the letters and diaries of John Cowper Powys (Cecil Woolf) and a collection of essays by Llewelyn Powys titled *A Struggle for Life* (Oneworld Classics).

Holly Howitt is a writer and academic, originally from Wales. She writes poetry, novels and short fictions, as well as academic articles, and is Senior Lecturer at Portsmouth University. She is currently completing a collection of poetry and a novel.

Notes on Contributors

G. Heath King, Ph.D, is a psychoanalyst and formerly taught interdisciplinary studies at Yale University. He is author of *Existence, Thought, Style: Perspectives of a Primary Relation, Portrayed Through the Work of Søren Kierkegaard*. He explored the philosophical foundations of psychology at the University of Freiburg, Germany where he completed his doctorate. Dr. King has written several articles applying psychoanalysis in understanding the relation between the formative experiences, words, and policies of world leaders, and predicting their course of action. Among these are Obama, Gaddafi, and Kim Jong-un. He has also decoded the psyche of notable mass murderers and terrorists of our time. He has recently presented a new paradigm fusing psychology and emerging technology to identify terrorists and preempt their designs.

Simone Kotva lives in Cambridge, where she is pursuing a doctorate in philosophical theology. In her spare time she writes, goes on fenland excursions, and helps organise the literary events of the Stockholm-based music festival O/MODERNT. Among her current projects are a children's story, and two collaborative projects on aesthetics written with the Tasmanian artist Susan Henderson and British violinist Hugo Ticciati.

Edward Lucie-Smith was born in 1933 at Kingston, Jamaica. He moved to Britain in 1946, and was educated at King's School, Canterbury and Merton College, Oxford. He is now an internationally known art critic and historian, who is also a published poet and a practising photographer. He has published more than a hundred books in all, chiefly but not exclusively about contemporary art. A number of his art books are used as standard texts throughout the world. Among the languages in which they have appeared are Chinese, Arabic and Farsi.

Ian Madden's short fiction has appeared in the *Edinburgh Review, New Writing Scotland, Wasafiri* and has been broadcast on BBC Radio 4.

Priscilla Martin teaches English Literature and Classics at Oxford. She has also taught at the Universities of Edinburgh, London and California. She is the author of *Piers Plowman: the Field and the Tower* and *Chaucer's Women: Nuns, Wives and Amazons* and co-author of *Iris Murdoch: A Literary Life*.

Derwent May has recently published a collection of poems, *Wondering About Many Women*, and his book on Proust, originally in the Oxford Past Masters series, has been republished (both from Greenwich Exchange). He was formerly literary editor of the *Listener* and the *Sunday Telegraph*.

David McVey worked for many years at the University of the West of Scotland and has taught Creative Writing for the Open University. He has published around one hundred short stories, a number of academic papers and non-fiction that focuses on history and the outdoors. He enjoys hillwalking, visiting historic sites and supporting his hometown football team, Kirkintilloch Rob Roy FC.

Jeffrey Meyers, a Fellow of the Royal Society of Literature, has recently published *Samuel Johnson: The Struggle* (2008), *The Genius and the Goddess: Arthur Miller and Marilyn Monroe* (2009), *George Orwell: Life and Art* (2010) – his fifth work on Orwell – and *John Huston: Courage and Art* (2011). Thirty of his books have been translated into fourteen languages and seven alphabets, and published on six continents. In 2012 he gave the Seymour lectures on biography, sponsored by the National Library of Australia, in Canberra, Melbourne and Sydney.

Mary O'Shea has won several prizes for short fiction, notably a Hennessy Literary Award, a Willesden Herald First Prize and Second Prize in *The London Magazine*. Her work has appeared in a number of journals and anthologies. She lives in Cork and is currently putting the finishing touches to her debut collection.

Sanjeev Sethi is author of two well-received books of poetry. He has worked in the media industry and at different phases of his career has written for various newspapers, magazines and journals. He has also produced radio and television programs. He lives in Mumbai.

George Tardios helped to found the Arvon Foundation's first writing centre as well as the Arvon Poetry Competition. He was a member of the General Council of the National Poetry Centre, and started the National Poetry Competition. In Tanzania he retraced, on foot, H. M. Stanley's 1871 journey in search of Dr. David Livingstone – a trek that took two years to complete. His poetry is published in various Arts Council and PEN Anthologies, the Puffin Book of *Salt Sea Verse*, and a textbook for schools, *English For Me*. He continues to write poetry, whilst embarking on an acting career, and has recently completed a collection, *Buttoned-Up Shapes* based on his mother's Cypriot village.